Interpreting Psychological Test Data

Interpreting Psychological Test Data

Associating personality
and behavior with responses
to the Bender–Gestalt,
Human Figure Drawing,
Wechsler Adult Intelligence Scale,
and the Rorschach Ink Blot Tests

Joseph Gilbert, Ph.D.

Volume II
Behavioral Attribute Antecedent

VNR VAN NOSTRAND REINHOLD COMPANY

NEW YORK   CINCINNATI   ATLANTA   DALLAS   SAN FRANCISCO
LONDON   TORONTO   MELBOURNE

IN MEMORIAM

Katherine Jennings Gilbert

April 15, 1925—September 5, 1979

Van Nostrand Reinhold Company Regional Offices:
New York Cincinnati Atlanta Dallas San Francisco

Van Nostrand Reinhold Company International Offices:
London Toronto Melbourne

Library of Congress Catalog Card Number: 77-20593.
ISBN: 0-442-25324-9

Manufactured in the United States of America

Published by Van Nostrand Reinhold Company
135 West 50th Street, New York, N.Y. 10020

Published simultaneously in Canada by Van Nostrand Reinhold Ltd.

15 14 13 12 11 10 9 8 7 6 5 4 3 2 1

Library of Congress Cataloging in Publication Data

Gilbert, Joseph, 1920-
    Interpreting psychological test data.

    "Associating personality and behavior with responses
to the Bender-Gestalt, human figure drawing, Wechsler
adult intelligence scale, and the Rorschach ink blot
tests."
    Bibliography: v. 1, p.
    Includes index.
    CONTENTS: v. 1. Test response antecedent.—v. 2.
Behavioral attribute antecedent.
    1. Personality assessment.   2. Bender gestalt test.
3. Draw-a-person test.   4. Wechsler adult intelligence
scale.   5. Rorschach test.   I. Title.
BF698.4.G46   155.2'8   77-20593
ISBN: 0-442-25313-3 Vol. 1
ISBN: 0-442-25324-9 Vol. 2

Introduction

Volume II of *Interpreting Psychological Test Data* presents the material from the first volume in reverse sequential order. Whereas Volume I presents test response first, followed by dynamic interpretation of that response ("Test Response Antecedent"), Volume II presents interpretation first as behavioral attribute or diagnostic syndrome, followed by the test response that suggests the interpretation ("Behavioral Attribute Antecedent").

The rationale and criteria for the content of the book remain as discussed in Volume I, as do the reference sources contained in the bibliography.

One aspect of this volume that differentiates it from the first is that reversal of the sequential order necessarily obscures the character of an interpretation as an alternative in most cases rather than as a distinct, independent entity. In Volume I the test response is usually followed by a variety of alternative interpretations or behavioral attributes the test response suggests. In Volume II presenting each separate interpretation as behavioral attributes isolated from the others associated with the test response separates it from its collective state and gives it an exclusive character that it often does not possess. Clinicians should be aware of this and determine from Volume I when necessary all the correlates of the test response.

I want to thank Judith M. Clair, R.N., for her meticulous and discerning scrutiny of a significant portion of the manuscript, which much enhanced its accuracy and clarity. The majority of the manuscript was typed with intelligence and resourcefulness by my daughter, Armida Gilbert, whose fortitude in deciphering my interlineated interlineations was awesomely resolute. I am grateful to both for their patience and support.

JOSEPH GILBERT

Contents

Interpreting Psychological Test Data

Part I
Bender-Gestalt Test

Adjustment

Adequate functioning, although other indications may suggest a lower maturational level:

Well-articulated circles, figure 2. (Hutt, 1969)

Good adjustment in children:

Orderly sequence. (Hutt, 1969- Clawson)

Defenses

Attempt to control affective stimuli:

Change of circle columns, design 2, to the vertical plane or reverse direction; rotation of upright hexagon of design 7 of more than $5°$ but less than $20°$ to the left. (Tolor-Schulberg-Story)

Compulsive doubting:

Crowding remaining designs on page after most of room on page is utilized. (Hutt, 1969)

Compulsivity:

Extreme orderliness of sequence. (Hutt, 1969)

Indecision:

Crossing difficulty at juncture of figures 4, 5, 6. (Hutt, 1969)

Inhibition:

Small figures. (Anderson-Halpern)

Overcontrol:

Increased angulation. (Hutt, 1969)

Possible denial:

Reduction of curve amplitude or of number of curves. (Hutt, 1969)

Possible isolation:

Reduction of curve amplitude or of number of curves, figure 6. (Hutt, 1969)

Regression:

Fragmentation or separation of open square and curve, figure 4. (Hutt, 1969)

Repression:

Reduction of curve amplitude or of number of curves. (Hutt, 1969)

Diagnostic Syndromes

ADDICTION
Alcoholics or alcoholic tendency:

Design 6 as non-intersecting separate lines; design 7 hexagons drawn as separate and not overlapping; rotation of upright hexagon of design 7 more than $5°$ but less than $20°$ to the left (Hutt, 1969—Story); elaboration of figure 6 to resemble water (Hutt, 1969; Tolor-Schulberg-Story); asymmetry; rotation; tremor (Tolor-Schulberg-Kaldegg); change of circle columns, design 2, to the vertical plane or reverse direction; drawing components of figure 7 as separated or with tips in contact. (Tolor-Schulberg-Story)

CHARACTER DISORDER
Characteristic of character disorders:

Low incidence of rotations. (Tolor-Schulberg)

Malingering psychopath antisocial personality ("psychopath"):

Placement of design A in lower left or lower right-hand corner. (Hutt, 1969)

NEUROSIS
Depression or depressive tendency:

Dip in figure 1; displacement of curve downward, figure 4; extension downward of curve on one side, figure 5 (Anderson-Halpern); decreased curvature; figure 1 dots drawn in downward angle to left; figures 2 and 3 lower at right end than left; mild clockwise rotation. (Hutt, 1969)

Neuroticism:

Crossing difficulty, especially designs 6 and 7; irregular sequence; marked isolated size change; mild angulation difficulty; mild curvature difficulty; mild rotation; movement in deviant direction; overly methodical or irregular sequence; very heavy, very light, or inconsistent quality (Hutt, 1969); inconsistent direction of lines (Hutt and Briskin; Tolor-Schulberg); change in size of angulation, curvature, or design parts; closure difficulty; excessive margin; irregular or overly methodical sequence (Tolor-Schulberg-Hutt); abnormal first figure placement; mild rotation (especially with depressives). [Tolor-Schulberg-Hutt and Briskin]

Phobic tendency:

Crossing difficulty at juncture of figures 4, 5, 6. (Hutt, 1969)

Substantial depressive tendency:

Clockwise rotation of first three figures. (Hutt, 1969)

PSYCHOSIS
Borderline psychosis:

Placement of design A in lower left or lower right corner page. (Hutt, 1969)

Manic state:

Confused sequence of Bender-Gestalt drawings (right to left instead of left to right, bottom to top instead of top to bottom, or some combination of these) [Hutt, 1969]; fanciful elaboration and ornamentation of the design; noncryptic embellishment. (Bender)

Paranoia:

Margin-based drawings. (Hutt, 1969)

Paranoid features:

Overextension of projection from circle, figure 5. (Hutt, 1969)

Paranoid schizophrenics:

Narrow margin. (Hutt, 1969)

Paranoid tendency:

Adding facial features to curves, figure 6. (Hutt, 1969)

Possible alcoholic psychosis or traumatic psychosis following head injury:	Rotation. (Bender)
Possible schizophrenia:	Fragmentation; perseveration. (Bender)
Psychosis:	Marked perceptual rotation. (Hutt, 1969)
Psychotics with manic tendency:	Doodling and elaboration. (Tolor-Schulberg-Hutt and Briskin)
Regressed schizophrenic:	Inability to correct rotation. (Hutt, 1969)
Response atypical of schizophrenics unless intense anxiety is present or the condition is incipient:	Margin-based drawings. (Hutt, 1969)
Schizophrenia:	Crowding (Anderson-Halpern); displacement of whole patterns; rotation 45° (Bender); component elements of figure drawn as separate (with intervening space) and with no effort at joining; confused sequence of Bender drawings (right to left instead of left to right, bottom to top instead of top to bottom, or some combination of these); doodling and elaboration; fragmentation; marked closure difficulty; marked curvature difficulty; moderate rotation, usually with capacity to correct; narrow margin (paranoids); perseveration; placement of design A in lower left or lower right page corner; redrawing of total figure; several pages required (prepsychosis); severe elaboration; severe perseveration; unawareness of rotation; very abnormal placement of first figure (Hutt, 1969); displacement of whole patterns (Tolor-Schulberg-Bender); rotation. (Tolor-Schulberg-Griffith and Taylor; Hutt and Briskin)

Schizophrenia, especially hebephrenics:	Primitive gestalt forms. (Hutt, 1969)
Schizophrenia, with chronicity:	Simplification. (Hutt, 1969)
Schizophrenia (with regression):	Primitive gestalt forms. (Hutt, 1969)
Toxic psychosis:	Confused sequence of Bender drawings (right to left instead of left to right, bottom to top instead of top to bottom, or some combination of these). (Hutt, 1969)

Intellectual Status

Increases as intelligence decreases:	Probability of rotations. (Tolor-Schulberg-Griffith and Taylor)
Retardation:	Change in angulation; collision tendency; component elements of figure drawn as separate (with intervening space) and with no effort at joining; doodling and elaboration; flattened curvature; fragmentation on figure 7 and 8; irregular sequence; marked closure difficulty; markedly irregular use of space; mild simplification; rotation. (Hutt, 1969; Tolor-Schulberg-Griffith and Taylor)

Norms

AGE PROGRESSIONS-DEVELOPMENTAL LEVEL (Chronological sequence rather than alphabetical)	
Nine-month to a year developmental level:	Ability to scribble imitatively. (Bender-Gesell)
One-year developmental level:	Ability to mark with a pencil. (Bender-Kuhlman norms)
One-to one-and-a-half-year developmental level:	Ability to scribble spontaneously. (Bender-Gesell)

Two-year developmental level:	Ability to imitate vertical stroke. (Bender-Gesell)
Two-year developmental level:	Circle copying. (Bender-Gesell)
Four-year developmental level:	Ability to copy square and triangle. (Bender-Gesell)
Four-year developmental level:	Circle copying. (Bender-Buckler)
Four-year developmental level:	Cross copying. (Bender)
Seven-year developmental level:	Age at which rotation ceases. (Tolor-Schulberg)
Seven-year developmental level:	Diamond copying. (Bender)
Ten-year developmental level:	Ability to reproduce complex design from memory. (Bender-Stanford-Binet)
Eleven-year developmental level:	Age at which all designs are accurately reproduced. (Bender)

BENDER'S OWN AGE
PROGRESSIONS for
CHILDREN (Chronological
sequence rather than alphabetical)

Children at three-year developmental level and under:	Scribble. (Bender)
Children at four-year developmental level:	Square copying. (Bender)
Children at five-year developmental level:	Star copying. (Bender)

ALPHABETICAL ARRANGEMENT
FOLLOWS FOR LAST TWO
ENTRIES

Ages 15-50, at least ten years of education:	Ranges in which age and education have an effect on Bender-Gestalt. (Tolor-Schulberg-Pascal and Suttell)
At least average intelligence:	Angles, diamonds, and oblique lines correctly rendered. (Bender)

Organicity

Adjoining occipital in temporal-parietal region; Wernicke's area or adjoining, probably left except in left-handed; closer to occipital the lesion, the greater the gestalt disturbance:

Probable area most involved in visual-motor gestalt functions. (Bender)

Alexia, aphasia:

Inability to recognize previously learned configurations, such as square, circle, and so on. (Bender)

Chronic alcoholic hallucinatory states:

Gestalt preserved, outlines indefinite. (Bender)

Brain damage (intracranial pathology, organicity):

Dashes or lines for dots; distortion of curves; inability to copy angles (Anderson-Halpern); change in angulation; collision; component elements of figure drawn as separate (with intervening space and with no effort at joining); decreased angle (rotation of circle columns toward vertical, figure 2); doodling; elaboration; fragmentation; fragmentation or separation of open square and curve, figure 4; inability to correct rotation; incoordination; margin-based drawing; marked angulation difficulty; perseveration on figures 1 and 2; redrawing of total figure; severe rotation, especially when subject does not recognize rotation or is unable to correct it; simplification; unawareness of rotation (Hutt, 1969); gross distortion and perseveration; poor coordination (Hutt and Briskin-Mosher and Smith); rotation (Tolor-Schulberg-Griffith and Taylor; Hutt and Briskin); breakdown of gestalt. (Tolor-Schulberg-Halpern)

Brain-damaged children:

Angulation difficulty; curvature difficulty; gross distortion. (Hutt, 1969–Weimar)

Brain-damaged retarded children:

Design 7 hexagons drawn as separate and not overlapping; omission of major part of at least one design (especially figure 7); perseveration (more on figure 1 than 2). [Tolor-Schulberg-Baroff]

Diffuse brain damage:

Overlapping difficulty. (Hutt, 1969)

Incidence greater for epileptics than for other organics:

Incidence of rotations. (Tolor-Schulberg-Hovey with Graham-Kendall test)

Neurologic condition:

Tremors. (Hutt, 1969)

Possible alcoholic psychosis:

Tremulous line. (Bender)

Possible dementia paralytica (chronic syphilitic meningoencephalitis):

Separation of parts (fragmentation), perseveration of gestalt. (Bender)

Possible occipital lesion:

Inability to localize objects in space and separate them from their background. (Bender)

Reading problems of children:

Incorrect number of units in designs 1, 2, 3, 5, 6. (Tolor-Schulberg-Clawson)

Traumatic psychosis following head injury:

Tremulous line. (Bender)

With other signs, possible dementia paralytica (chronic syphilitic meningoencephalitis):

Rotation with perseveration of gestalt. (Bender)

Symptomatology

Affect display and emotional disorganization, as in hebephrenics:

Curvilinear distortion. (Tolor-Schulberg-Guertin)

Ambivalence:

Atypical sequence. (Hutt, 1969)

Ambivalence toward same-sex parent:

Slight clockwise rotation tendency. (Hutt, 1969)

Anxiety:	Crowding remaining designs on page after most of room on page is utilized; excessive margin; poor coordination; margin-based drawings; placement of design A in extreme upper left-hand corner of page, especially with size reduction; placement of designs in upper left-hand corner (Hutt, 1969); excessive margin. (Tolor-Schulberg–Hutt and Briskin)
Anxiety relative to figures of authority:	Increase in height (vertical plane) of figures. (Hutt, 1969)
Anxiety and insecurity producing compulsive tendency:	Vertical placement of figures, each below the preceding figure. (Anderson-Halpern)
Blocking:	Crossing difficulty at juncture of figures 4, 5, 6. (Hutt, 1969)
Conflict over aggressive drives:	Difficulty with curved figures. (Hutt, 1969)
Conflict over authority figures:	Vertical placement of figures, each below the preceding figure. (Hutt, 1969)
Conflict with women:	Change of position, figure 8; closure difficulty of diamond, figure 8, male subjects; difficulty in joining diamond to side of hexagon, figure 8, male subjects. (Hutt, 1969)
Confusional state:	Reversal of design 45° or to mirror image of self. (Bender)
Constriction accompanying depression:	Decreased curvature. (Hutt and Briskin; Tolor-Schulberg)
Decreased emotionality:	Decreased curvature; increased angulation. (Hutt, 1969)
Depressive tendency:	Slight clockwise rotation tendency. (Hutt, 1969)
Detachment from others:	Large space between figures. (Anderson-Halpern)

Difficulty in interpersonal relationships; need to relate with social anxiety:	Lateral elongation (stretching out) of figures. (Hutt, 1969)
Difficulty in maintaining adequate interpersonal relations:	Closure difficulty. (Hutt, 1969)
Difficulty in maintaining interpersonal relationships; possible withdrawal:	Gaps in closure. (Hutt, 1969)
Disorganization:	Fragmentation. (Tolor-Schulberg-Guertin)
Dissociation:	Fragmentation. (Tolor-Schulberg-Guertin)
Emotional disturbance:	Closure difficulty; curvature difficulty on figures 4, 5, 6. (Hutt, 1969)
Externalized hostility:	Heavy pressure. (Hutt, 1969)
Feelings of castration and femininity in male; vaginal symbols:	May be evoked or suggested by circles. (Tolor-Schulberg-Hammer)
Flattening of affect tendency:	Flattening of curves (Anderson-Halpern); flattening of curve, figure 4; flattening of curve, figure 6. (Hutt, 1969)
General emotional imbalance, as with catatonics:	Unstable closure. (Tolor-Schulberg-Guertin)
Heterosexual anxiety:	Change of position, closure difficulty of diamond, figure 8, male subjects; difficulty in joining diamond to side of hexagon, figure 8, male subject. (Hutt, 1969)
Homosexual tendency:	Drawing components of figure 7 as separated or with tips in contact. (Tolor-Schulberg-Story)
Hostile acting out:	Irregular curvature with increased curvature. (Hutt, 1969)
Hostility externalized:	Heavy line, impulsive execution. (Anderson-Halpern)

Impulse control impairment: Change in angulation. (Hutt, 1969)

Inadequacy feelings: Crowding remaining designs on page after most of room on page is utilized; poor coordination. (Hutt, 1969)

Inadequacy feeling with effort at self-control: Excessive margin. (Tolor-Schulberg-Hutt and Briskin)

Inappropriate assertion: Crowding. (Anderson-Halpern)

Inhibited or internalized anxiety: Very light pressure. (Hutt, 1969)

Inhibition followed by impulsivity: Small figures or elements within a figure, alternating with large. (Anderson-Halpern)

Insecurity: Accentuated or sharpened angles; margin-based drawings; figures confined to upper half of page (Anderson-Halpern); extension of circular portion of figure 5; margin-based drawings. (Hutt, 1969)

Intense anxiety: Tremors. (Hutt, 1969)

Intensely anxious neurotics: Primitive gestalt forms. (Hutt, 1969)

Intense overt anxiety: Doodling and elaboration. (Hutt, 1969)

Interpersonal aggression on Rorschach, children as subjects: Closure difficulty. (Tolor-Schulberg-Clawson)

Interpersonal conflict: Elongation laterally of figure 2, correct number of circles. (Hutt, 1969)

Lack of confidence: Margin-based drawings, figures confined to upper half of page. (Anderson-Halpern)

Lack of spontaneity, possibly with withdrawal or flattened affect tendency: Reduction of number of curves or curve amplitude, figure 6. (Hutt, 1969)

Loss of control: Collision. (Hutt, 1969)

Lower motivational level: Decreased angle (rotation of circle columns toward vertical), figure 2. (Hutt, 1969)

Marked anxiety:	Collision. (Hutt, 1969)
Masculine striving:	Enlargement of square only, figure A; increased size of diamond, figure 8. (Hutt, 1969)
Masculine striving with felt masculine inadequacy:	Larger square than circle, with reduced size of square, figure A. (Hutt, 1969)
Prepsychosis:	Several pages required. (Hutt, 1969)
Primitive gestalt forms:	Dashes for dots, dots for circles (Hutt, 1969); separation of parts of design. (Tolor-Schulberg-Schilder)
Problem with authority:	Decrease in height of total figure, shortening of extension, figure 5; extension of vertical sides, open square of figure 4. (Hutt, 1969)
Problem with control of hostility:	Spiked curves, figure 6. (Hutt, 1969)
Psychopathology:	Accentuated or sharpened angles (Anderson-Halpern); fragmentation. (Hutt, 1969)
Psychotic factor:	Fragmentation. (Tolor-Schulberg-Guertin)
Reading difficulty in children:	Rotation of horizontal gestalt to the vertical place. (Hutt, 1969; Tolor-Schulberg-Fabian)
Reduction of affect expression (blandness):	Decreased angle (rotation of circle columns toward vertical), figure 2. (Hutt, 1969)
Rigidity alternating with impulsivity:	Careful execution, exaggeration of curves. (Anderson-Halpern)
Severe disturbance of association functions:	Doodling and elaboration. (Tolor-Schulberg–Hutt and Briskin)
Severe psychopathology:	Overlapping difficulty; primitive gestalt forms; rotation of figure. (Hutt, 1969)

Social anxiety:	Closure difficulty; decreased lateral size of figure 1; elongation laterally of figure 2, correct number of circles; nonintersecting curves, figure 6. (Hutt, 1969)
Suicidal rumination:	Intrusion of design 6 into design 5. (Hutt, 1969–Sternberg)
Tension:	Fine tremor. (Hutt, 1969)
Timidity:	Placement of designs in upper left-hand corner. (Hutt, 1969)
Transitional disturbance:	Awareness of rotation. (Hutt, 1969)
Unresolved need for sustaining interpersonal associations:	Left to right placement of figures. (Hutt, 1969)
Withdrawal:	Decreased lateral size of figure 1; decreased lateral size of figures; gaps in closure; placement of design A in extreme upper left-hand corner of page, especially with size reduction (Hutt, 1969); gaps (Tolor-Schulberg–Hutt and Briskin); design 6 drawn as nonintersecting separate lines; drawing components of figure 7 as separated or with tips in contact. (Tolor-Schulberg-Story)
Malingering:	Addition of more complex elements. (Tolor-Schulberg–Blum and Nims)
Possible malingering:	Absence of perseveration in presence of distortions atypical of diagnostic syndromes, correct rendition of parts with change of their relationship and direction; simplification of drawing with correct slant. (Bender)

Traits

Acting-out tendency:	Increase in size of circles of figure 2 progressively. (Hutt, 1969)

Aggressive drives: Collision of curved figures. (Hutt, 1969)

Attitude toward one's phallic sexuality: Significance of figure 8. (Tolor-Schulberg–Suzcek and Klopper)

Attitude toward regularity and importance of detail: Significance of figure 1. (Tolor-Schulberg–Suzcek and Klopper)

Basic sexual identification: Significance of figure 5. (Tolor-Schulberg–Suzcek and Klopper)

Concept of one's adequacy: Significance of figure 7. (Tolor-Schulberg–Suzcek and Klopper)

Dependence: Extension of circular portion of figure 5. (Hutt, 1969)

Egocentricity: Crowding (Anderson-Halpern); clockwise movement of angulation of circle columns progressively, figure 2; figure 1 dots lower on ends than in middle; figure on each page in center; rotation 90° to 180°. (Hutt, 1969)

Emotional instability: Dashes or lines for dots, distortion of curves; exaggeration alternating with flattening of curves; small figures or elements within a figure, alternating with large; variable spacing between columns, figure 2 (Anderson-Halpern); extra loop at terminus of curve, figure 4. (Hutt, 1969)

Emotional lability: Blunted or rounded angles (Anderson-Halpern); difficulty with angles; increase of curvature. (Hutt, 1969)

Feminine identification: Curve of figure 6 larger than square. (Hutt, 1969)

Handling of instinctual drives: Significance of figure 3. (Tolor-Schulberg–Suzcek and Klopper)

Immaturity: Atypical sequence. (Hutt, 1969)

Impulse control disorder: Doodling and elaboration. (Hutt, 1969)

Impulsivity:	Blunted or rounded angles; dashes for dots; exaggeration of curves; large space between figures (Anderson-Halpern); circles varying from loops to ovals, incorrect number of columns, figure 2; extra loop at terminus of curve, figure 4; increase in size of circles in figure 2 progressively; overlapping of circle, design A (Hutt, 1969); curvilinear distortion. (Hutt, 1969; Tolor-Schulberg-Guertin)
Inadequacy:	Margin-based drawing. (Hutt, 1969)
Inadequate impulse control:	Irregular sequence. (Hutt, 1969)
Increased affectivity:	Increase of angle of circles, figure 2. (Hutt, 1969)
Increased emotionality:	Decreased angulation. (Hutt, 1969)
Instability:	Large space between figures. (Anderson-Halpern)
Lack of empathy:	Crowding. (Anderson-Halpern)
Lack of spontaneity:	Increased angulation. (Hutt, 1969)
Low frustration tolerance:	Design 6 drawn as nonintersecting separate lines. (Tolor-Schulberg-Story)
Marked egocentricity:	First figure in center of page. (Hutt, 1969)
Narcissism:	Clockwise movement of angulation of circle columns progressively, figure 2; figure 1 dots lower on ends than in middle; one figure on each page, in center. (Hutt, 1969)
Negativism:	Right to left placement. (Hutt, 1969)
Oppositional tendency:	Counterclockwise rotation; large space between figures; one figure on each page, in center; rotation more than 180°. (Hutt, 1969)

Passive-dependent needs: Intrusion of one part into another. (Tolor-Schulberg)

Passive tendency: Difficulty with straight line figures. (Hutt, 1969)

Passivity: Difficulty with intersecting figures; difficulty with straight line figures; increased curvature; light line drawings; reduction of vertical dimension. (Hutt, 1969)

Problems of impulse control: Simplification. (Hutt, 1969)

Reaction to ambivalence and incongruities within self and its emotional experiences: Significance of figure 4. (Tolor-Schulberg)

Rebelliousness: Atypical sequence; right to left placement. (Hutt, 1969)

Rigidity: Rotation $90°$ to $180°$; severe perseveration. (Hutt, 1969)

Unpredictability: Variable spacing between columns, figure 2. (Anderson-Halpern)

Way individual copes with primitive instinctual drives or their derivatives: Significance of figure 6. (Tolor-Schulberg–Suzcek and Klopper)

Willingness to comply with externally imposed orderliness: Significance of figure 2. (Tolor-Schulberg–Suzcek and Klopper)

Part II
Human Figure Drawing

Adjustment

Absence of thought disorder; adequate reality contact:

Normal succession in drawing. (Anderson-Machover)

Criteria for retained reality contact:

Ability appropriately to evaluate psychotic-looking drawing when asked to "criticize it." (Hammer-Levy)

Good prognosis:

Persistence with drawing despite difficulties. (Hammer-Beck)

Improved prognosis for successful treatment of obesity:

Obese patients who draw slim figures. (Hammer)

Attitude

Contemptuous attitudes; tendency to think in terms of derisive social stereotypes.

Nose broad, flared, hooked. (Hammer-Levy)

Disdain:

Trim eyebrow. (Machover)

Prevailing attitude and mood:

Facial expression. (Machover)

Diagnostic Syndromes

ADDICTION
Alcoholics:

Figures tiny, well-depicted features. (Machover)

Alcoholism possibly:

Mouth emphasized. (Machover)

CHARACTER DISORDER
Aggressive psychopath with feelings of inadequacy:

Large figure shifted to left. (Machover)

Antisocial personality ("psychopath"):
Clothing foppish (overclothed); hands in pockets; large size drawing (large figure) [Machover]; excessive pressure (heavy pressure).   [Hammer-Payne; Hammer-Pfeister; Machover]

Body narcissism:
Same-sex figure nude and carefully rendered. (Hammer-Levy)

Caution:
Features masklike. (Hammer)

Delinquent tendency possibly:
Aggressive content, as daggers, guns, spears. (Hammer)

Dependency:
Arms long, weak (Anderson-Machover); arms overextended (Machover); breast area emphasized (Machover); buckle (Anderson-Machover); buttons (Hammer-Halpern; Hammer-Levy; Machover); buttons on clothing over breasts of figure (Hammer-Levy); circular strokes (Hammer-Alschuler and Hattwick); concave mouth (Machover); drawing near margin (Hammer); less than five fingers (Hammer); midline emphasis (Machover); mouth markedly full, open, or oval (Hammer-Levy); navel (Anderson-Machover; Hammer-Halpern, children as subjects); pockets. (Machover)

Egocentricity:
Body emphasis (underclothed) [Machover]; clothing carefully rendered (Hammer-Levy); clothing foppish (overclothed) [Machover]; eye a circle (no pupil) [Anderson-Machover]; left side of page figure (Machover); same-sex figure nude and carefully rendered. (Hammer-Levy)

Egocentricity (children as subjects):
Centered drawing. (Hammer-Alschuler-Hattwick)

Egotism:
Doodling of subjects name. (Hammer)

Explosive personality ("emotional instability"):
Body line reinforced; varied pressure. (Anderson-Machover)

Immaturity:

Body omitted (no trunk)—appendages attached to head (Machover); buttons (Hammer-Levy); clothing carefully rendered (Hammer-Levy); eye a circle (no pupil) [Anderson-Machover] ; grape fingers (Machover); neck omission (Machover); same-sex figure nude and carefully rendered (Hammer-Levy); younger figure than subject (Hammer); yo-yo. (Hammer-Levy)

Impulsivity:

Fluctuating pressure (Hammer-Levy); short strokes.   (Hammer-Alschuler and Hattwick)

Inadequacy with compensatory fantasy:

Features overemphasized. (Machover)

Infantile social behavior:

Features childlike. (Machover)

Lack of impulse control:

Neck omission. (Machover)

Narcissism:

Doodling of subject's name (Hammer); emphasis on curves in depicting body (Anderson-Machover); hair given much attention (Hammer); large-size drawing. (Hammer-Levy)

Inadequacy:

Buttons (Hammer-Levy); hands omitted (Hammer); very faint line. (Hammer)

Passive-aggressive ("oral aggressive"):

Mouth heavy-line (Machover); single-line mouth (Hammer-Levy); teeth shown.   (Hammer-Levy; Machover)

Passive-dependent ("oral-dependent"):

Breast emphasis male subject (Hammer-Levy); mouth concave, oral receptive. (Machover)

Primitive character structure:

Body omitted (no trunk)—appendages attached to head. (Machover)

Schizoid:

Body emphasis (underclothed) [Machover] ; ear emphasized or enlarged (Machover); eye closed (Machover); facial expression self-preoccupied (Machover); feet and hands dim or omitted (Machover); hair on jaw (Machover); hand dim or omitted (Machover); joint emphasis (Machover); knuckle emphasis (Machover); midline emphasis (stressed midline) [Machover] ; neck long (elongated) [Hammer-Levy] ; stance tight. (Machover)

Self-absorption:
Eye small. (Machover)

Self-indulgence:
Neck short, thick.
(Anderson-Machover)

Oral-eroticism:
Mouth markedly full, open or oval.
(Hammer-Levy)

Orality:
Mouth open. (Hammer)

Passive trend possibly:
Opposite-sex figure longer.
(Hammer-Levy)

NEUROSIS
Apprehensive neurotics
(apprehension with neurosis):
Faint line (Hammer-Pfeister); body line heavy. (Machover)

Deep depression:
Figures micrographic, with detail shading, erasures, pressure variations. (Machover)

Depression (depressed state):
Acceptance of task with minimal protest, good initial performance followed by obvious fatigue and discontinuation of task (Hammer); arms omitted (Machover); clouds (Anderson-Machover); excessive symmetry (Hammer); feet and legs drawn first (Hammer-Levy); inadequate detailing (Hammer); low on page drawing (Machover); narrow neck (Hammer-Levy); very faint line. (Hammer)

Discouragement:
Legs and feet drawn first.
(Hammer-Levy)

Egocentric hysteric:
Eye a circle (no pupil).
[Anderson-Machover]

Hysteric tendency:	Active same-sex figure (Hammer-Levy); fading line. (Machover)
Neurotic depression:	Figures micrographic, with detail shading, erasures, pressure variations. (Machover)
Neurotic tendency possibly:	Erasures. (Machover)
Obsessive-compulsive:	Buttons inconspicuous (as on cuffs); shoelaces, wrinkles, other unnecessary detailing. (Hammer-Levy)
Obsessive element accompanying dependency:	Buttons on cuffs. (Machover)
Significant depression:	Inability to complete drawing, marked paucity of details. (Hammer-Levy)

PSYCHOSIS

Auditory hallucinations:	Ear emphasized or enlarged. (Machover)
Auditory hallucinations in paranoid:	Ear emphasized or enlarged. (Anderson-Machover)
Catatonics:	Faint line. (Hammer-Pfeister)
Chronic schizophrenia:	Faint line. (Hammer-Pfeister)
Compulsive body image problem, as in early schizophrenia:	Fingers, fingernails, joints carefully depicted. (Hammer-Levy)
Depersonalization:	Robot for male figure (male subject). [Hammer]
Depersonalization fears:	Heavy thick lines. (Machover)
Feeling of body disorganization:	Features masklike; mask. (Hammer)
Involutional patients:	Figures tiny, well-depicted features (Machover); nose large. (Hammer-Levy)
Manic tendency (manic):	Active same-sex figure (Hammer-Levy); large centered figure (Machover); organs shown. (Hammer-Levy)
Paranoid:	Claw fingers (Machover); ear emphasized or enlarged (Anderson-Machover); excessive pressure (Hammer-Payne); eye a dot with pressure, unenclosed

Anderson-Machover); eye emphasized (Machover); eyes large, staring (Hammer-Levy); large grandiose figure (Machover); large head (Machover); marked symmetry (Machover); spear fingers (Machover); talon fingers. (Machover)

Paranoid grandiosity: Large centered figure. (Machover)

Paranoid possibly: Ear emphasized or enlarged. (Machover)

Preschizophrenic possibility: Off-balance figure. (Hammer)

Psychotic tendency: Body distortions (Hammer-Levy); disconnected lines, displaced parts (Hammer); profuse, smudgy shading. (Hammer)

Schizophrenia: Bizarre details (Hammer-Levy; Machover); confusion of full face and profile (profile forehead and nose, full-face eyes and mouth) [Machover]; ear emphasis (Machover); failure to recognize grotesqueness of drawing (Machover); features primitive, tiny (Machover); gross disproportion (Machover); internal organs shown (Machover; Hammer-Levy); joint emphasis (Machover); knuckle emphasis (Machover); neck like giraffe (Machover); omission of arms (Machover); organs shown (internal anatomy) [Hammer-Levy; Machover]; sex organs shown (Machover); unaware of grotesqueness of drawing (Machover); unessential detail emphasized (Machover); very faint line. (Machover)

Regressed schizophrenic: Figures tiny, primitive features. (Machover)

Simple schizophrenic: Teeth shown. (Machover)

Withdrawn schizophrenic: Very faint line. (Machover)

Somatic delusions: Organs shown (internal anatomy). [Machover; Hammer-Levy]

Thought disorder possibly: Head drawn last.   (Hammer-Levy)

Somatization

Asthmatic: Arms long and thin, mouth omitted. (Machover)

Feeling of decline associated with advancing age: Full bodies with shaded or thin legs (shaded legs may be homosexual anxiety). [Machover]

Hysterical swallowing inhibition: Neck long (elongated).   [Hammer-Levy]

Low energy: Light lines (Hammer-Levy); light pressure.   (Hammer–Alschuler and Hattwick)

Somatic delusions: Internal organs shown.   (Anderson-Machover)

Somatic preoccupation: Buttons in midline. (Hammer-Levy)

Defenses

Change is defense against spontaneous reaction to situation as symbolized by detail first depicted: Change of detail in drawing. (Hammer)

Compensation for felt inadequacy (male subject):   Shoulders massive on male. (Machover)

Compensatory fantasy: Hat clearly indicated, dim line body or no body. (Hammer-Levy)

Compensatory fantasy aggrandizement: Drawing that fills the page. (Hammer)

Compulsivity: Detailing   (Hammer-Levy);   over-symmetrical drawings (Machover); re-working, with addition of excessive detail. (Hammer-Levy)

Constriction: Figure miniscule, light line pressure (Hammer); minute detailing (Hammer-Waehner); rigid posture.   (Hammer)

Conversion or somatic preoccupation:	Midline emphasis (stressed midline). [Machover]
Fantasy activity:	Figure depicted in motion. (Anderson-Machover)
Inhibition (inhibited subjects):	Length of stroke movement increases (Hammer-Mira); neck long, thin (Machover); seated figure. (Hammer)
Intellectualization:	Excessive symmetry. (Hammer)
Isolation:	Right to left strokes (Hammer-Levy); unbroken, reinforced lines outlining figure. (Hammer-Levy)
Obsessive-compulsive:	Shoelaces, wrinkles, other unnecessary detailing (Hammer-Levy); excessive symmetry (Hammer); excessive detail. (Hammer; Machover)
Perfectionism:	Measurement lines or stick frame. (Machover)
Regression:	Body omitted (no trunk); appendages attached to head (Machover); hat plus buttons (Machover); eye a circle (no pupil) [Anderson-Machover] ; hair on female, not on male (Machover); hat, no clothes (Machover); hat on nude figure (Hammer-Levy); infrequent erasure (Machover); long fingers (Machover); trunk incomplete (Machover); upper left-hand corner drawings. (Buck)
Possible regression:	Mouth emphasized. (Machover)
Repression:	Light pressure (Hammer–Alschuler and Hattwick); neck thin (Machover); reinforced line, particularly with reference to area reinforced. (Hammer)
Withdrawal:	Features dim, with emphasis on head contour (Machover); hands omitted (Hammer); tiny drawings. (Hammer)
Withdrawal tendency:	Inadequate detailing. (Hammer)

Intellectual Status

Mental retardation ("mental defective")	Confusion of full face and profile (profile forehead and nose, full-face eyes and mouth) [Machover]; body omitted (no trunk) — appendages attached to head. (Machover)

Norms

Age factor in figure size:	Decreased size of figure more common in men over 30 and women over 40. (Hammer-Lehner and Gunderson)
Three to four years of age:	Head and limbs, little or no trunk. (Hammer-Halpern)
Four to five years of age:	Navel. (Hammer-Levy)
Five years of age:	Sexual differentiation of figures (Hammer-Halpern); ability to draw recognizable picture of a man. (Bender-Gesell)
Five to six years of age:	Hands and fingers. (Hammer-Halpern)
Six years of age:	Arms connected to trunk rather than head. (Hammer-Halpern)
Six to seven years of age:	Row of buttons. (Hammer-Halpern)
Eight years of age:	Change from segmented to unit body; shoulders; two-dimensional arms and legs. (Hammer-Halpern)

Object Relations

Affectional deprivation:	Buttons on clothing over breasts of figure (Hammer-Levy); pocket. (Hammer-Machover)
Anxiety over interpersonal relations:	Hands shaded. (Hammer)
Children; also adults preoccupied with past who are unable to emancipate themselves from their parents:	Parental figures rather than self-image. (Hammer)

Conflict over interpersonal relations:	Head drawn last. (Machover)
Dependency on opposite sex:	Chin emphasized on opposite sex. (Machover)
Desire for affection:	Arms overextended, reaching. (Machover)
Difficulty with interpersonal relations:	Hands hidden. (Hammer-Levy)
Female regarded as sexually rejecting:	Hand of female figure in pelvic area, male subject. (Hammer)
Hostility toward women, expressed overtly:	Witches. (Hammer-Levy)
Ideal self-perception of others; self-portrait:	Type of person drawn. (Hammer)
Identification with mother possibly:	Buttons on clothing over breasts of figure. (Hammer-Levy)
Identification with parent of same sex:	Older figure than subject. (Machover)
Lack of closeness in family situation:	Figures far apart in drawing a family picture. (Hammer)
Maternal dependency:	Buttons (Anderson-Machover); buttons in midline (Machover); joint or knuckle emphasis (Hammer); male receiving something of value from female (Hammer); maternal figure rather than female sex object (male subject) [Hammer] ; midline emphasis (stressed midline) [Machover] ; pocket (Anderson-Machover); torso of female upper half emphasized. (Machover)
Maternal dependency and domination:	Breast emphasis, female figure, male subject. (Anderson-Machover)
May express attitude subject feels other people have toward him, rather than his attitude toward them:	Facial expression. (Hammer)
Maternal figure:	Skirt ankle length on female, male subject. (Machover)

Maternal figure unnurturing:

Breasts small. (Machover)

Maternal figure regarded as rejecting, unloving, unsupportive:

Hands omitted on female figure. (Hammer)

Need for affection, nurturing warmth:

Sun added to the HFD scene. (Hammer)

Need for emotional security and warmth:

Fireplace (with fire in it) before figure. (Hammer)

Nurturance needs:

Arms long, weak. (Anderson-Machover)

Opposite sex viewed as more powerful:

Opposite-sex figure larger. (Machover)

Opposite sex viewed as punishing:

Arms heavy, shaded, on opposite sex. (Machover)

Opposite sex viewed as smarter or as possessing greater social authority:

Head enlarged on opposite sex. (Hammer-Levy)

Opposite sex viewed as stronger:

Chin emphasized on opposite sex. (Machover)

Rejection by maternal or paternal figure of opposite sex:

Arms omitted or short arms on opposite sex. (Machover)

Scolding maternal figure possibly:

Mouth omitted on female figure. (Machover)

Strong attachment to or dependency on parent or person of the opposite sex:

Drawing opposite sex first. (Hammer-Levy)

Wish for protective maternal figure, male subject:

Arms long and hands prominent, female figure. (Hammer-Levy)

Organicity

Epileptics:

Heavy pressure. (Hammer-Pfeister)

Organicity:

Head malformed (Anderson-Machover); heavy pressure. (Hammer-Buck; Hammer-Pfeister)

Organicity (including retardates):

Excessive pressure. (Hammer-Payne)

Senile patients:

Figures tiny, well-depicted features. (Machover)

Somatic head symptoms:	Head enlarged. (Hammer-Levy)

Sexual Functioning

Aggressive use of sexual characteristics; coquettishness:	Emphasis on female sex characteristics, female subject. (Hammer-Machover)
Anal-erotic interests:	Smudgy shading (Anderson-Machover)
Anxiety over masturbatory guilt:	Hands shaded. (Hammer)
Anxiety over sexual needs possibly:	Hair emphasis with heavy shading. (Hammer-Machover)
Anxiety relative to sexual function:	Shading in sexual areas. (Hammer-Levy)
Autoeroticism:	Hand at genital area. (Machover)
Breast fixation:	V-neckline on female, male subject. (Machover)
Constricted erotic response (women):	Female sex characteristics underemphasized, female subject. (Hammer-Fisher and Fisher)
Coquettishness, seductiveness, self-display:	Lashes long. (Anderson-Machover)
Desire to be a woman; feminine identification (men):	Back of male figure to observer, male subject. (Hammer-Levy)
Doubts about virility with compensatory virility striving:	Beard, moustache, other facial hair (male subject). [Hammer-Levy]
Exhibitionism or exhibitionistic tendency:	Earrings (Hammer-Levy); full-face figure (Machover); measurement lines or stick frame for body (Machover); peanut man, stick figure in subject capable of more advanced drawing. (Anderson-Machover)
Fantasy relative to female genitalia:	Hat crease. (Hammer-Buck)
Feeling of emasculation anxiety or masculine insufficiency:	Area depicted as broken, cut, damaged, or otherwise impaired. (Hammer)
Feeling of masculine insufficiency and lack of virility:	Balding male figures; hair white on male figure (Hammer); shoulders

exaggerated or other masculine details. (Hammer-Levy)

Female protest, feminine role rejection:	Drawing of male first, female subject. (Machover)
Feminine identification with dominant mother:	Breast emphasis, female subject. (Anderson-Machover)
Feminine identification dealt with by narcissism and obsessive-compulsive mechanisms:	Hair parted in middle (Hammer-Levy); head split. (Hammer-Levy)
Femininity:	Horizontal stroke (Hammer-Levy); rounded lines. (Hammer-Krout)
Feminine tendency:	Circular strokes (Hammer–Alschuler and Hattwick); trunk rounded. (Machover)
Feminine tendency ("effeminacy"):	Emphasis on circles in depicting body (Anderson-Machover); ankles and wrists small; arms and legs tapering; curved lines on body of male; lips full on male; trunk rounded; wrists and ankles small. (Machover)
Genuine satisfaction in sexual role (female subject):	Average emphasis on female characteristics; neither over- nor under-emphasized. (Hammer)
Hand of female figure in pelvic area (male subject):	Female regarded as sexually rejecting. (Hammer)
Homoerotic conflicts:	Hands extended behind back in anal area. (Hammer)
Homosexual anxiety:	Pants transparent (legs show through). (Machover)
Homosexual trend:	Breast area emphasized (Anderson-Machover); buttock emphasis (Anderson-Machover); buttocks and hips on male figure unusually emphasized or large and rounded (Hammer-Levy); clothing detail elaboration (Anderson-Machover); drawing opposite sex first (Hammer-Levy); effeminate features

(Anderson-Machover); eyes and lashes large (Hammer-Levy); features effeminate, male subject (Anderson-Machover); features effeminate, tie emphasized (Hammer-Levy); hair given much attention (Hammer); high heel on male, male subject (Hammer-Machover); hip emphasis on male figure, male subject (Hammer-Levy); lashes on male (Hammer; Machover); trunk rounded, waist narrow, male subject. (Hammer-Levy)

Impotency:	Cane. (Anderson-Machover)
Inadequate virility:	Sparse, unpressured hair. (Machover)
Infantile or repressed sex drives:	Hair emphasis. (Anderson-Machover)
Involutional impotency:	Foot of male emphasized. (Machover)
Involutional resistance to sexual decline:	Cane. (Machover)
Involutional sex problems (male subject):	Body of lower area of female visible through transparent skirt. (Machover)
Limited sexual experience:	Female sex characteristics underemphasized, female subject. (Hammer–Fisher and Fisher)
Masculine assertion; or need for it:	Nose strong. (Anderson-Machover)
Masculine tendencies or masculinity:	Angular body (Anderson-Machover); trunk angular or square. (Machover)
Masculine or virility striving:	Adam's apple; a cane; cigarette; hair area; pipe; tie. (Machover)
Masturbatory fixation:	Yo-yo. (Hammer-Levy)
Masturbatory guilt:	Finger omitted or overextended (Anderson-Machover); hands hidden (Hammer-Levy); hands shaded. (Machover)
Masturbatory preoccupation:	Trouser fly. (Machover)
More extensive sex experiences up to promiscuity possibly (female subjects):	Female characteristics overstressed. (Hammer–Fisher and Fisher)
Overt sexual aggression:	Tie flying or swept out. (Machover)

Passive homosexual conflict or tendency:	Ear emphasized or enlarged. (Hammer-Levy)
Passive homosexual tendency:	Several pockets (male figure, male subject). [Hammer-Levy]
Phallic symbol:	Elongated anatomical areas. (Hammer)
Primitive oral-eroticism:	Straw, toothpick between lips. (Machover)
Primitive sexual behavior:	Hat transparent. (Machover)
Professional artists:	Sex organs shown. (Machover)
Psychosexual immaturity:	Joint or knuckle emphasis. (Hammer)
Rebellion against sexual mores:	Nude figure with sexual parts. (Hammer-Levy)
Sensuality or sensual needs:	Hair emphasis. (Hammer-Machover)
Sexual acting out ("sexual immorality"):	Hair mussed. (Machover)
Sexual conflict:	Buttocks emphasized (Machover); sexual anatomy area distorted or omitted (Hammer-Levy); shoulders wide on female. (Machover)
Sexual fantasies (male subject):	Body of lower area of female visible through transparent skirt. (Machover)
Sexual identification conflict:	Drawing opposite sex first. (Hammer-Levy)
Sexual immaturity:	Breast area emphasized. (Machover)
Sexual impotency:	Large nose. (Hammer-Levy)
Sexual inadequacy:	Handkerchief of coat pocket emphasized (Machover); rounded curves, small tie (Machover); tie. (Machover)
Sexual inadequacy possibly:	Beard, moustache, other facial hair (male subject). [Hammer-Levy]
Sexual inadequacy and preoccupation:	Phallic foot. (Machover)
Sexual preoccupation:	Body of lower area of female visible through transparent skirt, male subject (Machover); cigarette (Machover);

	earrings (Hammer-Levy); gun (Machover); tie, flying or swept out (Machover); trunk not closed at bottom. (Machover)
Sexual role conflict or confusion:	Adam's apple (on opposite sex, that sex regarded as not virile) [Machover] ; arm and leg distortion or reinforcement, left side, male subject, male figure (Hammer-Levy); legs masculine on female figure (Machover); opposite sex drawn first (Machover); refusal or reluctance to draw figure of opposite sex. (Hammer-Levy)
Somatic sexual dysfunction possibly:	Female characteristics underemphasized, female subject. (Hammer-Fisher and Fisher)
Sophisticated oral-eroticism:	Cigarette between lips; pipe between lips. (Machover)
Strong sexual drive associated with guilt, wish to be castrated:	Armless figure of male, male subject. (Hammer-Levy)
Unsatisfying erotic experience, female subject:	Female characteristics overstressed. (Hammer-Fisher and Fisher)
Virility symbol:	Hair emphasis (shaded). [Machover]
Voyeuristic tendency:	Clothing transparent (body visible) [Machover] ; eye small (Machover); idealized nude figures (Hammer-Levy); V-neckline on female, male subject. (Machover)
Voyeuristic tendency with guilt:	Eye large, no pupil. (Hammer-Levy)

Situational States

Analysands:	Sex organs shown. (Machover)
Aspiration exceeds opportunities; environment viewed as excessively constraining:	Figure too large for page. (Hammer-Machover)
Primitive cultural origin:	Confusion of full face and profile (profile forehead and nose, full-face eyes and mouth). [Machover]

Status Needs

Emphasis on possession and social prestige:	Clothing elaboration, grooming. (Machover)
Felt lack of status:	Disheveled, unkempt figure. (Hammer)
Need for greater status and recognition than subject feels he possesses:	Uniformed cowboy or soldier, male figure of male subject. (Hammer)
Need for social approval and dominance:	Clothing foppish (overclothed). (Machover)
Overconcern for material criteria for social status:	Clothing carefully rendered. (Hammer-Levy)
Unsatisfying social status:	Clothes ill-fitting. (Hammer)

Symptomatology

Adolescents with feelings of inadequacy or rejection:	Cartoon figure, clown. (Hammer-Levy)
Aggression externalized or overt:	Arms extended from body and overlong (Hammer-Levy); arms long (Hammer); claw fingers (Machover); eye emphasized (Hammer-Levy); hands emphasized (Hammer-Levy); long fingers (Hammer); spear fingers. (Machover)
Aggressive tendencies:	Angular body (Anderson-Machover); arms out with fists clenched (Machover); chin enlarged (Hammer-Levy); few curves, many sharp edges (Hammer-Wehner); figure clothed, with toes exposed (Machover); gun (Hammer); hands powerful (Hammer); heavy shading (Machover); heavy thick lines (Machover); knife (Hammer); large same-sex figure (Hammer-Levy); middle-of-page drawing (Machover); more than five fingers (Machover); powerful hands (Hammer); pressure (Machover; Anderson-Machover); shading (Mach-

over); shoulders squared (Hammer); stance wide (Hammer-Katz); straight lines (Hammer-Krout); strokes away from subject (Hammer-Levy); teeth well-defined (Hammer); weapons. (Hammer-Levy)

Anxiety:

Broken lines (Hammer-Buck); clouds (Anderson-Machover); erasures (Machover); reinforced line (Hammer-Buck); shading (Anderson-Machover; Hammer-Levy); short sketchy strokes (Hammer-Levy); sketchy lines (Hammer); small figures (Hammer-Wehner, Hattwick, Elkisch); uneven line pressure. (Machover)

Assaultiveness:

Arms of male figure large (Hammer-Katz); arms reinforced (Hammer-Katz); combination of firm, heavy, and light lines (Hammer-Katz); eye prominent (Hammer-Katz; Machover); eye reinforced (Hammer-Levy; Hammer-Katz); fingers, no hands (Hammer-Katz; Machover); fingers reinforced (Hammer-Katz); foot emphasized (Hammer-Katz; Machover); hair reinforced (Hammer-Katz); heavy line (Hammer-Katz; Machover); large arms (Hammer-Katz); large fingers (Hammer-Katz); legs of male figure large (Hammer-Katz); legs reinforced (Hammer-Katz); stance wide (Hammer-Katz); stick fingers. (Hammer-Katz; Machover)

Awareness of physical impulses with effort to control them:

Neck excessively large. (Hammer-Buck)

Ear injury or hearing disability:

Ear emphasized or enlarged. (Anderson-Machover)

Breaks in judgment:

Transparencies. (Machover)

Castration fears and wishes: Nose cut off. (Anderson-Machover)

Castration which may be projected on opposite sex: Nose shaded. (Machover)

Circumstantiality: Labeling. (Machover)

Compensation for felt guilt: Hands large. (Machover)

Compensation for felt guilt, indecision: Chin exaggerated. (Hammer-Levy)

Compensation for felt weakness: Hands large. (Machover)

Compensation for inadequacy, indecision, fear of responsibility (dim line elsewhere, fantasy compensation): Chin emphasized. (Machover)

Compliance: Puppet. (Hammer)

Conception of self as dependent, helpless, insignificant: Arms dangling by sides, entreating facial expression, tiny same-sex figure. (Hammer)

Concern about sufficiency of intellect (brain-damaged, retarded): Head enlarged. (Machover)

Conflict area: Erasures (Hammer-Levy; Machover); line break (Machover); omission (Machover); reinforced line (Hammer-Levy; Machover); shading. (Hammer-Levy; Machover)

Conflict relative to part: Distortion of that part (Hammer-Levy); omission of that part. (Hammer-Levy; Machover)

Criticality: Angular body. (Anderson-Machover)

Cyclothymic: Fluctuating pressure. (Hammer-Levy)

Defensiveness: Rigid posture. (Hammer)

Defensive restriction of activity: Rigid posture, profile figure. (Hammer-Buck)

Dejection: Shoulders drooping. (Hammer)

Denial or repression of physical drives (children as subjects): Body omitted (no trunk); appendages attached to head. (Hammer-Jolles)

Depersonalization fears: Body line heavy. (Machover)

Depressed mood:	Below midpoint drawings. (Hammer-Buck)
Desire to escape from situation:	Sitting on edge of chair. (Hammer)
Difficulty in social contact:	Arms pressed to sides. (Hammer)
Discouragement:	Feet or legs drawn first (Hammer-Levy); feet omitted (Machover); legs omitted. (Machover)
Dissatisfaction with self:	Disguise (clown, etc.) [Hammer] ; excessive erasure. (Hammer)
Disturbed symmetry:	Incoordination. (Machover)
Emotional dependence:	Small figures. (Hammer–Wehner, Hattwick, Elkisch)
Emotional exhaustion:	Reclining or seated same-sex figure. (Hammer-Levy)
Emotional fixation at age depicted, or wish to return to youth:	Younger figure than subject. (Machover)
Emotional immaturity:	Breast area emphasized. (Machover)
Emphasis on fantasy:	Horizontal stroke. (Hammer-Levy)
Emphasis on fantasy (children as subjects):	Head enlarged. (Hammer-Levy)
Evasion:	Abstract or stick figure (Hammer-Levy); hands behind back or in pockets (Machover); profile figure. (Machover)
Evasion of body problems:	Peanut man, snowman, stick man. (Machover)
Evasion of problems:	Resistance to drawing figure. (Anderson-Machover)
Excitable subjects:	Length of stroke movement decreases. (Hammer-Mira)
Extreme tension:	Heavy pressure. (Hammer-Buck)
Fantasy preoccupied:	Head enlarged. (Hammer-Levy)
Fantasy rather than reality satisfactions:	Elevation of drawing above midline. (Hammer-Buck)

Fatigability, possibly associated with depression:

Decreased pace and productivity as drawing continues. (Hammer)

Fear:

Sitting on edge of chair. (Hammer)

Fear of aggressive impulses:

Arms pressed to sides. (Hammer)

Feeling of anxiety or of inferiority relative to body functions:

Head clearly indicated, dim line body or no body. (Hammer-Levy)

Feeling of being controlled by outside forces:

Robot for male figure (male subject). [Hammer]

Feeling of discomfort and restriction:

Small figures. (Hammer–Wehner, Hattwick, Elkisch)

Feeling of domination by others:

Puppet. (Hammer)

Feeling of insignificance or lack of worth:

Figure miniscule, light line pressure. (Hammer)

Feelings of inadequacy:

Below midpoint drawings (Hammer-Buck); disturbed symmetry (Machover); small same-sex figure (Hammer-Levy); tiny drawings. (Hammer)

Nose large. (Hammer-Levy)

Felt inadequate male role in adolescents, with striving for adequate male role:

Felt subjection to strong environmental pressure or stress, with fear of psychosis:

Strong wind in scene of Human Figure Drawing. (Hammer)

Forced amiability:

Mouth clownlike. (Machover)

Good prognosis:

Pathological Rorschach, less pathological drawing. (Hammer)

Grandiosity:

Size of drawing large. (Hammer)

Guilt:

Arms omitted (Machover); hands behind back or in pockets (Machover); shoulders drooping. (Hammer)

Guilt (as masturbation or theft):

Shaded fingers. (Machover)

Guilt over aggression:

Hands shaded. (Machover)

Helplessness:

Less than five fingers. (Hammer)

Hyperactivity:

Vertical stroke. (Hammer-Levy)

Ideas of reference:

Ear emphasized or enlarged (Machover);

	eye a dot with pressure, unenclosed. (Anderson-Machover)
Hostility:	Gun (Hammer); jagged lines (Hammer-Krout); knife. (Hammer)
Impaired self-esteem:	Facial scars on same-sex figure. (Hammer)
Improved prognosis:	Less pathology suggested by drawing than by Rorschach. (Hammer)
Inappropriate affect:	Mouth Clownlike. (Machover)
Indecisiveness:	Curvilinear line interrupted (Hammer-Levy); excessive erasure. (Hammer)
Infantile aggression:	Fingers, no hands; stick fingers. (Machover)
Infantile traits:	Grape fingers; petal fingers. (Machover)
Insecurity:	Abstract or stick figure (Hammer-Levy); breast emphasis (Machover); broken lines (Hammer-Buck); buttons (Machover); facial expression placating (Hammer-Machover); feet small, male subject (Anderson-Machover); finger-less hands (Machover); grape or petal fingers (Machover); ground line (Hammer-Machover); high-on-page figure (looks adrift) [Machover]; indeterminate vacillating stroke (Hammer-Levy); lack of symmetry (Hammer); midline emphasis (Machover); reinforced line (Hammer-Buck); shoes shaded (Hammer-Levy); small figures (Machover); uneven line pressure. (Machover)
Intellectual aspirations (with possible grandiosity):	Head enlarged. (Hammer-Levy)
Internalized hostility, self-contempt:	Cartoon figure, clown. (Hammer-Levy)
Lack of assertion:	Circular strokes (Hammer–Alschuler and Hammer); rigid posture. (Hammer)

Lack of confidence:	Apolegetic of drawings (Machover); drawing near margin (Hammer); hands behind back or in pockets. (Machover)
Lack of confidence in productivity or social contact:	Hands dim. (Machover)
Lack of drive, energy, or vitality:	Drooping shoulders (Hammer); inadequate detailing (Hammer); reclining or seated same-sex figure. (Hammer-Levy)
Lack of perseverence:	Indeterminate, vacillating stroke. (Hammer-Levy)
Latent severe pathology:	Pathological drawing, less pathological Rorschach. (Hammer)
Less favorable prognosis:	More pathology suggested by drawing than by Rorschach. (Hammer)
Loneliness:	Sitting on edge of chair. (Hammer)
Low self-esteem:	Disheveled unkempt figure. (Hammer)
Machover indices differentiating assaultive from nonassaultive subjects, as confirmed by Katz:	Fingers without hands; foot emphasis; heavy line; prominent eye; stick fingers; wide stance. (Hammer)
May express evasion or negativism:	Stick figure. (Hammer)
Mistrust:	Sitting on edge of chair. (Hammer)
Need for defensive intellectual control (children as subjects):	Neck emphasis. (Hammer-Halpern)
Need for help or support:	Fence to lean on, ground line; left-to-right strokes. (Hammer-Levy)
Need for stability because of disturbance produced by a conflict:	Feet on base of page. (Hammer-Buck)
Obsessive control of aggression:	Fingers with carefully indicated joints and nails. (Machover)
Overideational subject:	Head enlarged. (Machover)
Passivity as defense against aggressive impulses:	Arms pressed to sides. (Hammer-Levy)
Poor adjustment:	Few curves, many sharp edges. (Hammer-Wehner)

Poor judgment:	Profile head and legs, full-face trunk. (Machover)
Possible expectation of aggression from environment:	Facial scars on same-sex figure. (Hammer)
Possible symbolization of psychic trauma:	Facial scars on same sex figure. (Hammer)
Pressure for motor activity:	Active same-sex figure. (Hammer-Levy)
Pride over intellect:	Head enlarged. (Machover)
Primitive aggression:	Nostrils. (Machover)
Problem with control of anger or primitive drives:	Collar tight; neck long (elongated). [Hammer-Levy]
Psychopathology of incipient kind:	Extreme discontinuity in drawing (as head, then feet; shoulders, then legs, etc.) [Hammer]
Regression:	Neck omission. (Machover)
Reluctance to reveal self:	Resistance to drawing figure. (Anderson-Machover)
Repressed aggression:	Fingers articulated carefully and cut off by line (Machover); fists clenched or closed (Hammer-Levy); mitten hand. (Machover)
Restlessness:	Active same-sex figure (Hammer-Levy); erasures. (Machover)
Rigid emotional controls:	Stiff posture. (Hammer-Levy)
Sadism:	Mouth heavy line (Machover); pressure (Machover); teeth shown. (Hammer-Levy)
Secretiveness:	Features masklike (Hammer); peanut man, stick figure in subject capable of more advanced drawing (Anderson-Machover); stylistic drawing, as caricatured, facetious, simplified. (Anderson-Machover)
Self-consciousness:	Face dim; head dim. (Hammer-Levy)
Self-distrustfulness:	Abstract or stick figure. (Hammer-Levy)

Sensitivity to attitudes of others:	Ear emphasized or enlarged. (Anderson-Machover)
Sensitivity to criticism:	Ears large. (Hammer-Jolles, children as subjects)
Shrunken ego:	Figures tiny, primitive features. (Machover)
Shyness:	Face dim. (Hammer-Levy)
Social anxiety with need for contact:	Profile head, full-face body. (Machover)
Social dependency:	Full-face view. (Machover)
Subject is castrating or views maternal or paternal figures as castrating:	Scissors fingers. (Hammer)
Submissiveness:	Emphasis on circles in depicting body. (Anderson-Machover)
Tension:	Arms close to body (Machover); Constricted stroking (Hammer-Levy); fluctuating line (Machover); left-side-of-page figure (Machover); stance unbalanced (Machover); thin elongated line. (Hammer)
Timidity:	Dim line (Machover); features dim with emphasis on head contour (Machover); self-conscious stance (Machover); sketchy lines. (Hammer)
Uncertainty:	Short, sketchy lines. (Hammer-Levy)
Unrealistic euphoria:	High-on-page figure. (Machover)
Unstableness:	Fluctuating pressure. (Hammer-Levy)
Voyeurism:	Transparencies. (Machover)
Weakness:	Horizontal stroke. (Hammer-Levy)
Withdrawal:	Arms omitted (Machover; Hammer-Levy); constricted stroking (Hammer-Levy); face turned toward page, so that back of head shows (Hammer); feet omitted (Machover); fingers articulated carefully and cut off by

line (Machover); legs omitted. (Machover)

Worst prognosis: Pathology about equally distributed in all drawings and in Rorschach. (Hammer)

Traits

Adaptability: Pressure variations. (Hammer-Pfeister)

Aloofness: Elevation of drawing above midpoint. (Hammer-Buck)

Ambition: Firm lines (Hammer-Levy); more than five fingers. (Machover)

Ambition for accomplishment or acquisition: Arms long. (Machover)

Assertiveness: Heavy pressure (Hammer); pressured lines (Anderson-Machover); straight-line strokes (children as subjects) [Hammer–Alschuler and Hattwick]; vertical stroke. (Hammer-Levy)

Caution: Features masklike; mask. (Hammer)

Concretisticness: Below-midpoint drawings. (Hammer-Buck)

Controlled behavior: Long strokes. (Hammer–Alschuler, children as subjects)

Decisiveness: Uninterrupted straight lines. (Hammer-Levy)

Determinedness: Vertical stroke. (Hammer-Levy)

Drive: Firm lines. (Hammer-Levy)

Emotionality: Centered drawing; circular strokes. (Hammer–Alschuler and Hattwick, children as subjects)

Energy: Heavy pressure. (Hammer)

Expansiveness: Large same-sex figure (Hammer-Levy); size of drawing. (Hammer)

Extroversion (environment-oriented): Left-to-right strokes (Hammer-Levy); right-side-of-page figure (Machover); strokes away from subject. (Hammer-Levy)

Feminine identification:	Emphasis on left side of figure. (Hammer-Levy)
Flexibility:	Pressure variations. (Hammer-Pfeister)
Introspection:	Head enlarged. (Hammer-Levy)
Introversion (self-oriented):	Left-side-of-page drawing (Machover); right-to-left strokes (Hammer-Levy); stroking in (toward the body). [Hammer-Levy]
Moodiness:	Varied pressure. (Anderson-Machover)
Need for autonomy:	Arms long and powerful; legs long. (Hammer-Jolles, children as subjects)
Optimism:	Drawing high on page. (Machover)
Pedantry:	Minute detailing. (Hammer-Waehner)
Perseverance:	Energetic, unhesitant stroke. (Hammer-Levy)
Physical power drive:	Broad shoulders. (Machover)
Poor judgment:	Transparency. (Anderson-Machover)
Presence of drive:	Persistance with drawing despite difficulties. (Hammer-Buck)
Rebellion:	Fists clenched or closed (close to body, repressed; out from body overt). [Machover]
Refinement:	Eyebrow trim. (Machover)
Relative freedom from anxiety:	Slight or minimal shading. (Hammer-Levy)
Responsiveness:	Rhythmic stroking. (Hammer-Levy)
Restraint:	Light pressure. (Hammer–Alschuler and Hattwick)
Secretiveness:	Mask. (Hammer)
Security:	Centered drawing (Hammer–Alschuler-Hattwick); energetic, unhesitant stroke. (Hammer-Levy)
Self-esteem:	Size of drawing. (Hammer)
Social accessibility:	Full-face figure. (Machover)

Social communication:	Full-face view. (Anderson-Machover)
Uninhibitedness:	Eyebrow bushy (Machover); rhythmic stroking. (Hammer-Levy)
Uninhibited impulse expression:	Neck short, thick. (Anderson-Machover)

Part III
Wechsler Adult Intelligence Scale (WAIS)

Adjustment

Inhibited normal subject (with other indices):

Even achievement; good overall Wechsler efficiency; nonimpulsive and nonpedantic to-the-point verbalization. (Schafer–Clincial Application)

Cognitive Functions

A test of abstraction or concept formation:

Similarities. (Rapaport)

Anticipation and planning ability:

Picture Arrangement. (Rapaport)

Does not necessarily imply no impairment of recent memory:

No decrement of Digit Span. (Rapaport)

Measure of attention:

Digit Span. (Rapaport)

Measure of concentration:

Arithmetic. (Rapaport)

Practical judgment:

Comprehension subtest. (Anderson–Mayman–Schafer–Rapaport; Rapaport)

Defenses

Avoidance tendency:

Breeziness, joking. (Schafer-Clinical Application)

Denial of serious personal problems:

Breeziness, joking. (Schafer-Clinical Application)

Doubt:

Overelaborate, overinclusive, or redundant responses. (Rapaport)

Indecision:

Overelaborate, overinclusive, or redundant responses. (Rapaport)

Intellectualization:	Increment Information; overelaborate, overinclusive, or redundant responses; Similarities increment (19+); Vocabulary increment, adequate Verbal. (Rapaport)
Projective trend:	High Arithmetic, Picture Completion, and Similarities. (Schafer-Clinical Application)
Repression in hysteroid states:	Neurosis with decrement Information below Comprehension. (Rapaport)
Repressive tendency:	Decrement of Information and Vocabulary (Anderson-Mayman-Schafer-Rapaport); Information below Comprehension and Vocabulary. (Schafer-Clinical Application)

Diagnostic Syndromes

ADDICTION
Alcohol addiction:	Easy items often missed; Vocabulary elevated, rest of Verbal and Performance reduced. (Schafer-Clinical Application)

CHARACTER DISORDER
Antisocial personality ("narcissistic character disorder"):	Clang associations on Vocabulary, impulsive guessing, supercilious attitude; evasive, facetious, pretentious; higher Digit Span than Arithmetic; Performance equal to or above Verbal, high Picture Arrangement, low Arithmetic. (Schafer-Clinical Application)
Antisocial personality ("narcissistic character disorder," "psychopath"):	Higher Performance than Verbal score; low Arithmetic. (Schafer-Clinical Application)
Antisocial personality ("psychopath"):	Deferential, ingratiating, pseudoconscientious (Schafer-Clinical Application); high Picture Arrangement, flippancy (Schafer-Clinical Application); high Picture Completion

(Schafer-Clinical Application); impulsive guessing, especially on Information and Vocabulary, good Block Design, high Digit Span, moralizing comments on Comprehension (Schafer-Clinical Application); low Comprehension and Similarities, Performance above Verbal, good visual motor speed and coordination, high Picture Arrangement, especially with schemers (Schafer-Clinical Application); Vocabulary definitions arbitrary, irrelevant. (Rapaport)

Blandness in antisocial personalities ("psychopaths"):

High Digit Span.   (Schafer-Clinical Application)

Character disorder:

Breeziness, joking; high Digit Span and Performance.   (Schafer-Clinical Application)

Character disorders, including antisocial personalities ("psychopaths") and addictions:

Decrement Picture Completion and Arithmetic, retained Picture Arrangement. (Rapaport)

Low anxiety tolerance and resistance to reflection, as with antisocial personality ("narcissistic character disorder"):

Incorrect solutions to Arithmetic, with assertion by subject that he guessed, when near correctness of response indicates that he did not. (Schafer-Clinical Application)

Paranoid personality ("paranoid condition"):

High Similarities, Arithmetic and Picture Completion; often-irrelevant details; overmeticulous verbalization; preoccupation with minutiae. (Schafer-Clinical Application)

Schizoid personality:

Concepts based on absence rather than presence of attributes (Schafer-Clinical Application); Digit Span equal to or above Arithmetic or Vocabulary (Rapaport); increment of Arithmetic and Digit Span (Rapaport); high Digit Span, low Arithmetic ("schizoid character") [Schafer-Clinical Application] ;

increment Block Design above Vocabulary and Performance means. (Rapaport)

NEUROSIS

Anxiety neurosis:

Difficulties in verbal expression, with anxious speech in broken phrases and trouble in remembering correct terms (may be decompensating obsessive-compulsive). [Schafer-Clinical Application]

Depression:

Decrement Block Design (Rapaport); decrement of Digit Symbol (Rapaport); decrement Information relative to Vocabulary (Rapaport); decrement Picture Arrangement below Vocabulary but not markedly below other Performance tests (Rapaport); giving up easily, lack of persistence (Schafer-Clinical Application); increment failures on easy items of Information, with increment passes on difficult ones (Rapaport); lack of qualification, elaboration, and verbal fluency; few peculiar verbalizations (even with psychotic depression); self-criticality; a few perceptual distortions in Picture Arrangement and Picture Completion for some psychotic depressives (Schafer-Clinical Application); low Arithmetic, Comprehension, Digit Span, and Similarities (Schafer-Clinical Application); low Digit Span and Object Assembly (Schafer-Clinical Application); low Performance score (Schafer-Clinical Application); Performance lower than Arithmetic and Information—the greater the reduction the greater the depression (Schafer-Clinical Application); Picture Arrangement decrement (Rapaport); Similarities decrement below Vocabulary (Rapaport); Similarities easy item failure (neurotic and psychotic depression) [Rapaport] ; Verbal high, Performance low (Rapaport); Vocabulary score generally above Performance. (Rapaport)

Hysterical neurosis (hysterical features, hysteria):

Comprehension higher than Information, high Performance subtest score (Schafer-Clinical Application); decrement Information below Comprehension (Rapaport); increment Information relative to Vocabulary (Rapaport); decrement Performance and Vocabulary, increment Picture Completion (Schafer-Clinical Application); high Digit Span and Performance (Schafer-Clinical Application); higher Performance than Verbal score (Schafer-Clinical Application); increment failures on easy items of Information, with increment passes on difficult ones (Rapaport); low Digit Span (Schafer-Clinical Application); moralizing content (Schafer-Clinical Application); Verbal I.Q. usually below superior range and may be borderline. (Schafer-Clinical Application)

Obsessive-compulsive neurosis (obsessives, obsessive-compulsive trend or tendency):

Decrement Comprehension below Vocabulary and Information (Rapaport); decrement Performance and Vocabulary, increment Picture Completion (Rapaport); high Information and Vocabulary, relatively low Comprehension and Performance, possible slight reduction of Similarities (Schafer-Clinical Application); increment of both Arithmetic and Digit Span (Rapaport); increment Information (Rapaport); increment Information and Vocabulary, decrement rest of Verbal tests (Rapaport); overelaboration (Anderson-Mayman-Schafer-Rapaport); Vocabulary increment, adequate Verbal. (Rapaport)

Organic brain syndrome:

Similarities decrement below Vocabulary. (Rapaport)

Phobia:

High Digit Span.
(Schafer-Clinical Application)

PSYCHOSIS
Acute schizophrenic episode or
chronic undifferentiated schizophrenia:

Decrement Arithmetic and Comprehension, retained Digit Span (Schafer-Clinical Application); failing easy Picture Completion (Rapaport); increment Information and Vocabulary, decrement rest of Verbal tests (Rapaport); low Object Assembly and Picture Completion (Schafer-Clinical Application); marked decrement of Digit Span (Rapaport); Vocabulary above all other Verbal scales (intellectual deterioration), retained Block Design and Object Assembly, low Digit Span, Picture Arrangement, and Picture Completion.
(Schafer-Clinical Application)

Acute paranoid schizophrenia:

Inertia and inability to concentrate on Arithmetic, with high Block Design and Object Assembly; Similarities high.
(Schafer-Clinical Application)

Chronic schizophrenia, especially
chronic paranoid schizophrenia:

Similarities low.
(Schafer-Clinical Application)

Chronic schizophrenic blandness:

High Digit Span, Object Assembly, and Digit Symbol (Schafer-Clinical Application); High Digit Span (Schafer-Clinical Application); increment Digit Symbol. (Rapaport)

Chronic undifferentiated schizophrenia
("chronic schizophrenia"):

Blandness, inappropriate affect (Schafer-Clinical Application); circumlocutious and irrelevant verbalizations, devious associations (Schafer-Clinical Application); inability to say Digit Span backward (Rapaport); inappropriate affect or blandness (Schafer-

Clinical Application); low Picture Arrangement, Similiarities (Schafer-Clinical Application); missing easy Information items with average intelligence (Schafer-Clinical Application); reduced Vocabulary and Verbal (Rapaport); schizophrenia with large drop in Arithmetic and Similarities (Schafer-Clinical Application); Vocabulary score above Performance. (Rapaport)

Contraindicates chronic schizophrenia except paranoia:

Vocabulary score high. (Rapaport)

Contraindicates paranoia:

Vocabulary score low. (Rapaport)

Contraindicates psychotic depression:

Low Arithmetic, with good Comprehension. (Schafer-Clinical Application)

Incipient psychotic break:

Digit Span eight points or more below Vocabulary. (Schafer-Clinical Application)

Intellectualizing paranoids:

Decrement Picture Arrangement; decrement Picture Completion, increment Vocabulary and Verbal. (Rapaport)

Latent ("incipient") rather than acute schizophrenia; fantasies rather than delusions:

Good Wechsler and absence of schizophrenic verbalizations with evidence of apprehension and fantasy withdrawal. (Schafer-Clinical Application)

Latent schizophrenia ("incipient schizophrenia"):

Increment Information (Rapaport); increment Information, mild decrement Vocabulary (Rapaport); orderly Wechsler responses—there may be extreme drop of one subtest (especially Digit Span, Arithmetic, and Picture Completion), and occasional odd verbalizations (Schafer-Clinical Application); Vocabulary increment, adequate Verbal. (Rapaport)

Paranoia, with other indices:

Limited perceptual distortions in Picture Arrangement and Picture Completion. (Schafer-Clinical Application)

Paranoia ("paranoid condition"):   Ability to work effectively and appropriately; high Arithmetic, Picture Completion, and Similarities. (Schafer-Clinical Application)

Paranoid overalertness: High Arithmetic and/or Picture Completion in schizophrenic setting. (Schafer-Clinical Application)

Paranoid schizophrenia: High Block Design with general drop of Performance level (Schafer-Clinical Application); high Picture Completion and Similarities (Schafer-Clinical Application); low Performance plus low Similarities (Schafer-Clinical Application); Picture Arrangement and Picture Completion markedly below Block Design and Object Assembly, high Comprehension (Schafer-Clinical Application); relatively slight scatter (with much more scatter confusion) (Schafer-Clinical Application); retained Comprehension score (Schafer-Clinical Application); schizophrenia, well-retained Comprehension (Rapaport); well-retained Comprehension, low Performance and low Similarities. (Schafer-Clinical Application)

Paranoid syndromes: Adequate Verbal, Vocabulary increment. (Rapaport)

Paranoid tendency: Concern with what examiner writes down (Schafer-Clinical Application); distorted auditory and visual perceptions and misperceptions (Schafer-Clinical Application); evasiveness (Schafer-Clinical Application); increment Picture Completion (Rapaport); objection to examiner's verbatim recording of patient's spontaneous remarks (Schafer-Clinical Application); psychosis with decrement Information below Comprehension (Schafer-Clinical

Application); Similarities above other Verbal subtest scores (Schafer-Clinical Application); Similarities high (Shafer-Clinical Application); Similarities increment above Verbal and Vocabulary mean. (Rapaport)

Psychosis:

Decrement Comprehension below Vocabulary and Information; Vocabulary definitions arbitrary, irrelevant. (Rapaport)

Psychotic depression:

Decrement Block Design below impaired Performance; decrement Comprehension below Vocabulary and Information; decrement easy Arithmetic items; decrement Similarities below Vocabulary and Verbal mean, clinical evidence of depression; failing easy Picture Completion; increment Information and Vocabulary, decrement rest of subtest scores; large decrement of Digit Symbol; misses on easy Comprehension items; misses on easy Vocabulary; reduced Vocabulary and Verbal; Similarities easy item failure; Verbal markedly higher than Performance scores; very low Picture Completion; Vocabulary score above Performance. (Rapaport)

Psychotic tendency:

Vocabulary above other subtest scores. (Rapaport)

Regressed schizophrenics:

Decrement Digit Symbol. (Rapaport)

Schizophrenia:

Absurd and impulsive responses (Schafer-Clinical Application); associating to Vocabulary words (Schafer-Clinical Application); clang associations to Vocabulary items (Schafer-Clinical Application); confusion in identification of objects on Picture Completion with good intelligence

(Schafer-Clinical Application); decrement easy Arithmetic items (Rapaport); decrement Information relative to Vocabulary (Rapaport); decrement Picture Completion, otherwise retained Performance (Rapaport); Digits backward markedly superior to Digits forward (Schafer-Clinical Application); elevated Digit Span (Schafer-Clinical Application); extreme variability on and between subtests (Schafer-Clinical Application); fail-easy, pass-hard variability (Schafer-Clinical Application); failure on items patient should know by reason of training or interests (Schafer-Clinical Application); high Block Design with rest of Performance low (Schafer-Clinical Application); higher Digit Span than Arithmetic (Schafer-Clinical Application); inappropriate solutions (Schafer-Clinical Application); increment Block Design above Vocabulary and Performance scores (Rapaport); increment failures on easy items of Information, with increment passes on difficult ones (Rapaport); increment Object Assembly, decrement other Performance tests (Rapaport); irrelevancies (Schafer-Clinical Application); misses on easy Comprehension items (Rapaport); peculiar literalness (Schafer-Clinical Application); Picture Arrangement and Picture Completion markedly below Block Design and Object Assembly (Schafer-Clinical Application); reduced Arithmetic, Picture Completion (Schafer-Clinical Application); Similarities decrement below Vocabulary

	(Rapaport); wild guessing with high intelligence. (Schafer-Clinical Application)
Schizophrenia, especially paranoid schizophrenia:	Increment Digit Span backward above Digit Span forward. (Rapaport)
Schizophrenia, including paranoid schizophrenia:	Peculiar verbalizations. (Schafer-Clinical Application)
Schizophrenia (paranoid, simple and undifferentiated):	Similarities easy items failure. (Rapaport)
Schizophrenic tendency:	Digit Span equal to or above Arithmetic or Vocabulary; marked Verbal or Performance subtest scatter; peculiar distortion of Digit Symbol characters; Verbal subtests impairment. (Rapaport)
Simple schizophrenia:	Increment Information, mild decrement Vocabulary (Rapaport); I.Q. in average range or better, perceptual vagueness, wild bland guessing (Schafer-Clinical Application); high Digit Span—Information and Vocabulary may be low (Schafer-Clinical Application); higher Performance than Verbal score (Schafer-Clinical Application); low Arithmetic (Schafer-Clinical Application); low Picture Completion (Schafer-Clinical Application); low Verbal with good scores on Object Assembly and Digit Symbol (Schafer-Clinical Application); visual-motor coordination subtest scores higher than Picture Arrangement, Picture Completion, and Verbal—low Arithmetic and Comprehension. (Schafer-Clinical Application)

Situational States

Cultural deprivation:	Similarities decrement. (Rapaport)

Symptomatology

Anxiety:	Digit Span decrement below Vocabulary (Rapaport); Digit Span six or more points below Information (Schafer-Clinical Application); Picture Arrangement decrement (Rapaport); decrement of Digit Symbol. (Rapaport)
Blandness:	Increment Object Assembly, decrement other Performance tests (Rapaport); schizophrenia with high Object Assembly and Digit Span (Schafer-Clinical Application); wild guessing. (Anderson-Mayman-Schafer-Rapaport)
Blandness in hysteric:	High Digit Span. (Schafer-Clinical Application)
Confusion:	Extreme subtest scatter. (Schafer-Clinical Application)
Contraindicates depression:	Vocabulary score high. (Rapaport)
Contraindicates depression; suggests disorganization tendencies:	Circumlocutious, verbose verbalizations. (Schafer-Clinical Application)
Contraindicates obsessive-compulsive states:	Vocabulary score low. (Rapaport)
Impaired concentration:	Higher Digit Span than Arithmetic. (Schafer-Clinical Application)
Impaired judgment:	Decrement Comprehension below Information. (Rapaport)
Impulsivity:	Wild guessing. (Anderson-Mayman-Schafer-Rapaport)
Intellectualizing neurotics:	Picture Arrangement decrement. (Rapaport)
Low anxiety tolerance:	Higher Digit Span than Arithmetic. (Schafer-Clinical Application)
Maladjustment:	Decrement visual-motor coordination. (Rapaport)

Neurosis, including depression:

Decrement Arithmetic and Digit Span below Vocabulary, decrement Digit Span greater than decrement Arithmetic. (Rapaport)

Neurotic depression:

Clinical evidence of depression, increment of Similarities above Vocabulary. (Rapaport)

Neurotic tendency:

Performance lower than Verbal, mild Verbal scatter. (Rapaport)

Obsessive doubting:

Decrement Digit Symbol. (Rapaport)

Psychopathology:

Decrement of Information and Comprehension; marked scatter. (Rapaport)

Self-depreciating attitude:

"I don't know" responses to Comprehension. (Schafer-Clinical Application)

Tension:

Low Digit Span and Object Assembly (Schafer-Clinical Application); low Object Assembly (Schafer-Clinical Application); only Block Design and Object Assembly of Performance moderately low, rest adequate, especially if response is rapid. (Schafer-Rapaport)

Traits

Ideational tendency:

High Digit Span with neurosis. (Schafer-Clinical Application)

Intellectual striving:

Elevated scores on Information, Comprehension, and Vocabulary (Klopfer—Developments I); restricted formal education with high Information score—Comprehension and Information above Similarities and Vocabulary. (Schafer-Clinical Application)

May reflect inflexibility as well as impaired judgment:

Low Comprehension subtest score. (Rapaport)

Ostentatious, overmeticulous sophistication:

Pedantic response to WAIS, as "Carnivora," "mammals," "quadrupeds" with animals item of Similarities. (Rapaport)

Strict moral code:

High Comprehension score. (Schafer-Clinical Application)

Part IV
Rorschach

Acting-out Potential

Absence of conscious tension-reducing fantasy:
Hostility and sex themes, involving humans, without M. (Beck and Molish)

Acting out:
Absence of shading; "bug" content; only color C, especially when blood or fire to Card II or IX and in absence of M and shading (with M or longer record, perseveration of C); ink, paint content; recreation content; reduction R, mediocre W increment (Phillips and Smith); achromatic, one-half chromatic; C + CF greater than FC; form-minus color (Klopfer-Developments I); pure C (more than one). [Beck and Molish]

Acting out of assaultive tendencies:
Crab and lobster content. (Phillips and Smith)

Acting out, with felt inability to restrain oneself:
Explosion, volcanic eruption content. (Klopfer-Developments I)

Acting out of hostility:
Edging, shock, Card I (Phillips and Smith); explosion, red area; people fighting and bleeding; spearhead. (Schafer-Rorschach)

Acting- out impulsivity relatively unrestrained by social disapproval:
C + CF twice shading. (Klopfer-Developments I)

Acting-out tendency without excessive dependency:
C + CF greater than FC: 2 X texture. (Klopfer-Developments I)

Aggressive impulses (hostility):

Aggressive A, as lions, tigers; people in conflict (Klopfer-Davidson); amazon content; arrow content; blood content; bomb content; cannon content; cartoon woman; caveman content; charging bull; club content; crouching animals; demon content; devil content; hatchet content; horns content; Ku Klux Klan figures; Medusa content; menacing female figure; Prussian content; rifle content; savages content; saw content; shears content; shrew content; (Joseph) Stalin content; stinger content; torpedo content; volcano content (Schafer-Rorschach); animals fighting; mutilated content (Beck and Molish); derogatory remarks about the cards; destruction and mutilation content; mouth content; stain content (Phillips and Smith); overpoliteness (Rapaport); (H): Hd; lion, panther, tiger content (citing Goldfarb). [Klopfer-Developments I]

Aggressive response to frustrated dependency needs:

Gums and teeth content.
(Klopfer-Davidson)

Assaultiveness:

Absence FC; "bug" content; emphasis on recreation content; shock possibly on Cards I and II, the latter with special conditions; at least 2–3 M present, minimal or no C; pure C perseveration.
(Phillips and Smith)

Covert hostility:

Rough texture. (Phillips and Smith)

Defiance possibly:

Indian content. (Schafer-Rorschach)

Destructiveness (potential for destructive acting out):

Amazon content; arrow content; bomb content; cannon content; cavemen content; centaur content; charging bull; demon content; devil content; club content; hatchet content; horns content; Ku Klux Klan figures content; Medusa content; menacing female figures; Mr. Hyde (from *Dr. Jekyll and Mr. Hyde*); poison gas content; Prussian content; rifle content; savages content; saw content; shears content; shrew content; spear content; (Joseph) Stalin content; stinger content; torpedo content; volcano content (Schafer-Rorschach); blood content; color naming; denial of meaning in color; incidental references to color; stain content. (Phillips and Smith)

Destructiveness, possibly with anxiety:	Explosion content. (Schafer-Rorschach)
Direct expression of aggressive impulses:	"Splattered, splotch" content. (Schafer-Rorschach)
Dishonesty:	CF dominance. (Phillips and Smith)
Episodic aggressive behavior:	Edging, shock, Card II (men more than women). [Phillips and Smith]
Estrangement:	Low P. (Beck III)
Externalized hostility:	Aggressive A and H; color greater than M; caricatured or inanimate H; death, dehumanization, mutilation; extratensive experience balance with aggressive content and space percepts (Beck III); criticism of cards. (Schafer-Rorschach)
Externalization of responsibility:	Criticism of cards. (Schafer-Rorschach)
Failure to deal realistically with the environment:	Vague D. (Phillips and Smith)
Fear of impulses with inability to inhibit acting out:	Excessive qualification plus rapid initial response time. (Phillips and Smith)
Hostility, possibly with anxiety:	Explosion content. (Schafer-Rorschach)

Immature aggression:	Extratensive experience balance, increment S. (Beck III)
Immaturity:	A greater than 50%; arbitrary and inappropriate FY; bird content; cat content; chicken content; children's literature; H and (H) content; cockroach content; covering part of blot with hand to exclude nonpercept area; dragon content; edging, shock, Card VII; elephant content; excessive qualification plus rapid initial response time; FM (without compensatory M); frog content; inappropriate consistent turning, usually with R given to upright position; lackadaisical comments on mild disparity between response and blot outlines; low-form color; M in A; M in Hd; nongeneric storybook animals (bee, cat, chicken, duck, horse, rabbit, etc.); oral-aggressive FM; seahorse content; travel content; turkey content; underproduction of M; vague W (map, X-ray) [Phillips and Smith]; card VII popular human as animals or children; egg, nest content, center upper D, Card VI; genitalia increment (Klopfer-Developments I); fairy-tale entities; M in Hd (Beck and Molish); FM greater than twice the number of M if CF greater than FC; TF. (Klopfer-Davidson)
Immaturity with anticipation of rejection, frustrated dependency needs, impulsivity:	Bug (beetle) content. [Phillips and Smith]
Immaturity with id impulses pressing for immediate expression:	FM. (Klopfer-Davidson)
Impairment of external control:	Extratensive experience balance, increment space. (Beck III)
Impulsivity (impetuosity; impulsive acting out; impulsive, unreflective acts):	Abruptness; CF−; color > M; excessive qualification plus rapid initial response

time; low-form red, expressed dislike or hesitancy in use; perseverated,
unelaborated CF; pure C (more than
one); response time 5''; response
time 10'' or less (Phillips and Smith);
blood or fire content; C + CF greater
than FC; CF; CF greater than FC;
decrement M and FM; form-minus
color; FM equal to 2 X M; mediocre
or poor form; no H content; sum C
greater than 2M, FY greater than 3
(Klopfer-Developments I); C, CF; CF
and space increment; explosion content, red area; low-form color; people
fighting and bleeding; spearhead; T,
TF (Schafer-Rorschach); C, CF-; CF;
pure C (more than one) [Beck and
Molish]; CF; color greater than M;
decrement A; decrement F+ (Rapaport);
CF, immediate response to color on
cards II and III (Klopfer-Davidson);
F-, low-form color, rapid card turning, rapid speech, restlessness; increment CF; very rapid response time
for first response, color cards (Beck
III); no M or sharp form.
(Schafer-Clinical Application)

Inability to tolerate conscious anxiety: Edge interpretations. (Rapaport)

Increases chances of suicide: High intelligence with resignation.
(Beck and Molish)

Indirect aggression: Fire content. (Phillips and Smith)

Intolerance of fantasy: Decrement M. (Schafer and
Rorschach)

Irresponsibility: C + CF greater than FC; FM (without
compensatory M); recreation content
(Phillips and Smith); decrement FM
and M; mediocre or poor form (Klopfer-
Developments I); Eskimo content.
(Schafer-Rorschach)

Lack of common sense:	Decrement of populars (Anderson-Beck); poor form, rare Dd. (Klopfer-Davidson)
Lack of concern over acting out:	CF dominance. (Phillips and Smith)
Lack of inhibition:	Lack of qualification. (Beck and Molish)
Lack of insight (lack of insight into complexes, emotional experiences, or motivations):	Animals as first response, Card I (Phillips and Smith); decrement A, M, P, possibly with overemphasis on certain content categories (Beck III); edge interpretations (Rapaport); form-minus color without subjective discomfort (Klopfer-Developments I); hostility and sex themes, involving humans, without M. (Beck and Molish)
Lack of planning ability:	Responses 10″ or less. (Phillips and Smith)
Lack of secure self-control:	C, CF, T, TF (Schafer-Rorschach); lack of qualification. (Beck and Molish)
Lethargic but with impulsive acting-out potential:	Arbitrary and inappropriate FY. (Phillips and Smith)
Limited capacity for reflection and self-confrontation:	Evasion, vagueness. (Schafer-Rorschach)
Low anxiety tolerance:	Absence of shading (Schafer-Clinical Application); avoidance of shading or emphasis only on light rather than heavy shading; evasion, vagueness. (Schafer-Rorschach)
May imply ability to delay impulse gratification:	Form-determined F+. (Rapaport)
Morbid sadistic preoccupation:	Mutilation content. (Schafer-Clinical Application)
Narcissism (narcissistic tendency, possible narcissism):	Adornment associations and objects; CF and space increment; clothing content; dress-form content; exotic associations with the Arabian Nights;

gem content; hairdresser's headrest; jewelry content; low-form color; low-form color only (increment C + CF), no FC; nude or scantily dressed women (chorus girl, sunbather); orchid content; peacock content; perfume bottle content; pure C (more than one); vague low-form W's; volubility (Schafer-Rorschach); C + CF > FC (Schafer-Clinical Application); C + CF > FC; few shading, M, R; decrement passive M; decrement shading; impotency responses possibly; pure C (more than one); stated inability to produce a response.   (Phillips and Smith)

Narcissistic spontaneity possibly:

Emphasis on C and CF.   (Beck and Molish)

Narcissistic striving:

Vague low-form W's. (Schafer-Rorschach)

Need for immediate gratification:

Pure C (more than one).   [Phillips and Smith]

Negativism (oppositionality):

Automaton content; bleeding, crushed, mutilated animals, anatomy, and persons; botched or poorly prepared adornments, materials, and specimens; bowed, debased, powerless, slovenly, subjugated persons; brassiere content; breastplate content; burdened animals and people; carnivorous animals and insects; CF and space increment; cutting or squeezing implements; damaged, deteriorated, diseased animals, objects, persons, and plants; dead missing, or mutilated animal, human, or plant limbs; dragon content; drooping or limp limbs or organisms; emaciated or tattered figures (begger, scarecrow); fire and hell content; flat- or small-bosomed woman; fleeing, frightening, and sinister animals, figures, and places; guiding-beams content (beacon, lighthouse); helpless, powerless animals and figures; loss-of-grip associations; missing parts; performing animals and pets; rejection of cards; rejection of response after verbalized; scars and wound content; slave content; supporting objects; symbols of imprisonment; tattered figures; tortured persons; volubility (Schafer-Rorschach); C, CF associated with white space; literal content (Beck III); extratensive experience balance (Klopfer-Developments I); figure-ground reversal space; form poor, rare Dd; overcriticalness of card, use of white space (Klopfer-Davidson); increment space; schizophrenic space (Beck and Molish); space (Anderson-Beck; Rapaport; Schafer-Rorschach); space with increment color. (Rapaport)

Negativistic or oppositional reaction to anxiety:	Avoidance of shading on shading cards, with increment of white space on the cards. (Rapaport)
Oppositional behavior externalized:	Space in extratensive setting. (Beck and Molish)
Passive-dependency with suicidal gestures:	Edging, shock, Card I. (Phillips and Smith)
Poor judgment:	CF-. (Phillips and Smith)
Poorly controlled emotional impulses:	Blood content. (Klopfer-Developments I)
Primary narcissism possibly:	C, CF- increment; little or no FC, no M. (Beck and Molish)
Potential for sporadic impulsive acts:	One CF only color. (Schafer-Clinical Applications)
Provocative behavior:	Volubility. (Schafer-Rorschach)

Pyromania possibly:

Rebelliousness (resistiveness):

Resentfulness:

Resentment over frustrated
dependency with absence of
insight:

Sadism (sadistic impulses,
sadistic tendency):

Explosion, fire content. (Phillips and
Smith)

Decrement of populars; space (Anderson-Beck); Indian content; space (Schafer-Rorschach); low P (Beck III); increment space; schizophrenic space; (Beck and Molish)

Gums and teeth content. (Klopfer-Davidson)

Gums and teeth content. (Phillips and Smith)

Amazon content; color naming, poor form red; destruction and mutilation responses; storm content (Phillips and Smith); animals devouring other animals or persons; arrow content; attacking horned animals; biting and stinging animals and insects; blood content; bomb content; cartoon and virago women; cavemen content; charging bull; clawing animals; club content; colliding animals and limbs; coyote content; crab content (other than popular D1, D7, and D8 of Card X); crocodile content; crushing objects and military armament (tanks, steam roller); cutting or squeezing implements; deformed heads content; demon content; devil content; Dracula content; erupting lava content; explosions, mutilation, and weapon content; fangs content; flaming tail of jet plane or rocket; gas mask; gun content; hatchet content; horns content; humans in combat; Medusa content; menacing female figures; pliers content; Prussian content; pursuing animals; rhinoceros content; rifle content; savages content; saw content; shears content; shrew content;

spear content; (Joseph) Stalin content; stinger content; tapeworm content; tiger content; tomato worm content; torpedo content; vampire content; volcano content. (Schafer-Rorschach)

Sadism, possibly with anxiety:

Explosion content. (Schafer-Rorschach)

Sadistic impulses, especially if in space area:

Hammer content. (Schafer-Rorschach)

Sadistic preoccupation of a morbid kind:

Mutilation content. (Schafer-Clinical Application)

Sadomasochism:

Authoritative, supernatural, or threatening figures; bleeding rectum content; creature with talons around anus; elevated or low social status symbols; symbols of imprisonment; servant content; symbols of rebellion and revolution. (Schafer-Rorschach)

Severely impaired emotional control:

C, CF− increment; little or no FC; no M. (Beck and Molish)

Suicidal tendency (suicidal attempts, suicidal impulses, suicidal potential; suicidal rumination):

Canyon, chasm, cliff content; death content; decay content (including fungus) [Phillips and Smith]; C, CF with depressive material; drowning and hanging content; dysphoric mood; painful affect; religiosity, serenity, or tranquility associations; increment M with space increment; M in depression; M with vista in blend; tranquil landscape content. (Beck and Molish)

Suicidal tendency possibly, especially in intelligent persons who display painful affect:

Guns and knives, high places, lake or river bank, ropes. (Beck and Molish)

Temper:

Color naming, poor form red. (Phillips and Smith)

Tendency to react before reflecting:

Very rapid response time for first response, color cards. (Beck II)

Tenuous controls:

Increment aggressive destructive fantasy. (Schafer-Clinical Application)

Unreflectiveness:

Absence of shading; decrement M; pure C (more than one). [Rapaport]

Adjustment

Ability to recuperate from stress:

More than one response to cards, quick response, response to disturbing card areas. (Schafer-Rorschach)

Absence of incapacitating overt psychosis at the moment; some adaptive resources:

Absence of pure C, presence of FC, acceptable even if marginal F+ and P%. (Schafer-Rorschach)

Absence of manifest anxiety:

Antiquity content. (Phillips and Smith)

Absence of negativism:

X-ray content. (Phillips and Smith)

Acceptance and awareness of need for affection:

FT. (Klopfer-Davidson)

Accurate perception:

Increment F+. (Beck III)

Acquisition of self-control with retained freedom of self-expression:

M+. (Phillips and Smith)

Activity (active, active orientation):

Charging animals; dancing content; leaping content; motion content; playing content; fishing content; springing content (Schafer-Rorschach); decrement M, color greater than M; preference for warm colors. (Phillips and Smith)

Active striving for independence:

Octopus content; scarab content; scorpion content; spider content. (Phillips and Smith)

Adaptive resources (adaptability, adaptive potential):

Esthetic forms (snowflakes, etc.); FC content (Phillips and Smith); good-quality response on III and X, after poor-quality responses on II and IX, respectively; improved F+ quality on X after mediocre or poor-quality responses on VIII and IX. (Beck and Molish)

Adults of superior intelligence without emotional pathology:	Exceptionally low animal content. (Beck III)
Assertion:	Figure of authority (politican, etc.); personal pronouns. (Phillips and Smith)
At least minimal adaptability and emotional control:	Increment of optimum sum color FT, FY, with increment F+. (Schafer-Rorschach)
Awareness:	Optimal FT. (Klopfer-Davidson)
Awareness of impulses and acceptance of them:	FM equal to M. (Klopfer-Davidson)
Awareness of the proprieties:	P. (Beck and Molish)
Behavior that may be immature but is still socially acceptable:	FM greater than 2M; FC greater than CF. (Klopfer-Davidson)
Capacity for change:	Ambiequal experience balance, with increment of both color and M. (Beck and Molish)
Capacity for empathy:	M+. (Phillips and Smith)
Capacity for insight:	FV. (Klopfer-Davidson)
Capacity for at least partial insight:	FM. (Klopfer-Developments I)
Capacity to restrain impulses:	M+. (Rapaport)
Common sense:	Increment D, F+; optimum P. (Rapaport)
Complex personality with capacity for matter-of-fact attitude:	Color with high F%, M, shading. (Klopfer-Davidson)
Constructive fantasy and imagination:	Form-plus M. (Klopfer-Developments I)
Cooperativeness:	Laying card down after response. (Phillips and Smith)
Culture and social adjustment:	Antiquity content. (Phillips and Smith)
Degree of contact with reality:	Original responses. (Rorschach-*Psychodiagnostics*)
Dependent needs with insight:	Center D, Dd. (Phillips and Smith)

Desirable self-assertion and ego strength possibly:	Figure ground reversal space. (Klopfer-Davidson)
Drive:	Large number of R. (Beck and Molish)
Effective sublimation:	Increment M without psychopathology. (Rapaport)
Ego strength:	F+ content; M+. (Klopfer-Davidson); form-plus M; M greater than FM, FM, Fm at least half of M (Klopfer-Developments I); optimum space in normal personality structure. (Beck and Molish)
Ego strength, although neurotic problems may be apparent (or psychopathology may be present:	Color-denial, shading denial; FM+, Fm, and M+. (Klopfer-Developments I)
Emotional stability:	Form-plus M; good-form M in optimal relation with FM; good H content (Klopfer-Developments I); good-form red. (Phillips and Smith)
Extraversion:	Decrement M, color greater than M. (Phillips and Smith)
Favorable prognostic sign (favorable prognosis, positive prognostic sign):	Color shock; extensor M; FC; grossly deviant Rorschach responses interspersed with good-quality responses; improved F+ quality on X after mediocre or poor-quality responses on VIII and IX (Beck and Molish); remarks suggesting response is contingent and possible rather than certain. (Phillips and Smith)
Favorable prognostic sign for psychotherapy:	Ambiequal experience balance, with increment of both color and M. (Beck and Molish)
Favorable prognostic sign in schizophrenia:	Color shock (Beck and Molish); pleasantly toned color comments. (Phillips and Smith)
Favorable prognostic sign for successful adjustment (favorable prognosis):	Abstraction content. (Phillips and Smith)

Feeling of immaturity with adult responsibility:	Baby, child, infant content. (Phillips and Smith)
Freedom from pathology:	Laying card down after response. (Phillips and Smith)
Ideational with moderate feeling tone and superior intelligence:	Abstraction content. (Phillips and Smith)
Imagination:	Original responses. (Rorschach-*Psychodiagnostics*)
Independence:	Decrement color, good-form M. (Klopfer-Developments I)
Independence (or need for independence):	Extensor M. (Beck and Molish; Beck III)
Independence of thought:	M greater than average. (Phillips and Smith)
Industriousness:	Bee content. (Klopfer-Davidson)
Intact formal thought processes; if subject is psychotic, disturbance is limited to delusional material:	F+ on first response, Card I. (Phillips and Smith)
Intellectualizing normal:	Edge details. (Phillips and Smith)
Interest in good rapport with others:	Good FC+. (Schafer-Rorschach)
Liveliness:	Charging animals content; dancing content; leaping content; pushing content; springing content. (Schafer-Rorschach)
Mature adaptability:	Texture with other determinants. (Phillips and Smith)
Maturity:	FY with form-plus color; good-form red. (Phillips and Smith)
More favorable prognosis than Rorschach content might suggest:	Coherent language, grossly bizarre Rorschach associations. (Beck and Molish)
Normality (normals):	Absence blood content; absence card description; absence clothing content; absence Dd as first response to two or more cards; absence F– to card I, first

response; absence M in abstraction; absence pure C; absence religious content; absence stain content; even response, Card IX, increment R, Card X: fewer than three Hd; fewer than two art content, males; FC; FC greater than C + CF; FC equal to M (approximately); H equal to M approximately; nature content; no more than one (H); personal content; pleasantly toned shading; positive comments on color; presence of H; use of personal pronouns; totem pole content. (Phillips and Smith)

Normality, although guardedness may be present:	Ten responses plus. (Phillips and Smith)
Originality:	FY with form-plus color (Phillips and Smith); original responses (Rorschach-*Psychodiagnostics*); 0+. Klopfer-Davidson)
Poise:	W: M. (Phillips and Smith)
Positive assertion:	Optimum space in normal personality structure. (Beck and Molish)
Potential for accomplishment:	Antiquity content. (Phillips and Smith)
Potential for creativity:	Kinesthetic responses (M) (Rorschach-*Psychodiagnostics*); M+ (Klopfer-Davidson; Klopfer-Developments I); whimsical content. (Beck and Molish)
Potential for empathy:	M+. (Klopfer-Developments I)
Potential for flexibility:	Ambiequal experience balance, with increment of both color and M. (Beck and Molish)
Potential for good adjustment:	FC, FM, FV (Klopfer-Davidson); recovery on subsequent card after shock on previous card (Beck III); remarks suggesting response is contingent and

Potential for good social and vocational adjustment, but with residual passive-dependent wishes:

Potential for insight:

Potential for orderly procedure:

Potential for productive activity:

Practicality:

Productivity:

Realism:

Reality contact adequate:

Reality contact adequate to that degree:

Reality contact unimpaired:

Reality testing not necessarily impaired as might be the case if Dd were not high:

Recognition of individuality in others:

Resilience; adequate defense system despite anxiety trend:

Resistive tendencies within limits:

possible, rather than certain (Phillips and Smith); whimsical content. (Beck and Molish)

Bay, harbor content. (Phillips and Smith)

Form-plus M (Klopfer-Developments I); vista. (Phillips and Smith)

Orderly sequence. (Beck III)

High R (with other positive indices). (Beck and Molish)

Decrement A + P; increment F + D; increment A, D, orderly sequence (Beck III); increment D, F+ (Klopfer-Developments I); increment F + D (Rapaport); W at expectancy. (Phillips and Smith)

FY with form-plus color. (Phillips and Smith)

W at expectancy. (Phillips and Smith)

Adequate F + P, sequence; optimal A content. (Beck and Molish)

Rejection of poor-form percept. (Schafer-Rorschach)

Extended F+ 80–90%. (Schafer-Rorschach)

Dd high, F+ slightly below 65%. (Schafer-Clinical Application)

M+. (Phillips and Smith)

Initial avoidance or poor-form response to red areas, followed by form-plus response to red areas on card. (Schafer-Rorschach)

Further inquiries about turning card after permission is given. (Phillips and Smith)

Self-acceptance:	M greater than FM, FM at least half of M. (Klopfer-Developments I)
Self-assertion:	Extensor M (Beck and Molish); "I"; WM. (Phillips and Smith)
Self-control:	FM (+) equal to M greater than FM, few FM. (Klopfer-Developments I)
Self-respect:	Good -form M in optimal relation with FM; good H content (Klopfer-Developments I); "I"; personal pronouns. (Phillips and Smith)
Spontaneity:	CF. (Klopfer-Developments I)
Stability:	FC greater than C + CF; FC equal to M (approximately) [Phillips and Smith] ; FM (+) equal to M greater than FM, few FM. (Klopfer-Developments I)
Stability (if less than 3 FM):	M equal to or greater than FM + Fm. (Klopfer-Developments I)
Stable value system:	Personal pronouns. (Phillips and Smith)
Sublimatory striving; working out of anxiety in nonpathological fantasy activity and imagination:	Form-plus shading with M+. (Beck and Molish)
Successful adjustment but with fear of rejection from others:	Peninsula content. (Phillips and Smith)
Successful adjustment but with sensitivity to authority:	Aggressively active H (football player, etc.); Figure of authority (politician, etc.). [Phillips and Smith]
Suggests reality contact is still at least partially retained, although it may be deteriorating or impaired:	Qualification of bizarre responses. (Schafer-Rorschach)
Superior adjustment and intelligence if F+:	Astronomy content. (Schafer-Rorschach)
Tactfulness:	Optimal FT. (Klopfer-Davidson)
Tenacity:	Figure ground reversal space. (Beck III)
Unimpaired judgment when optimum:	F+. (Phillips and Smith)

With female subject healthy narcissism, good adjustment, high intelligence:

Clothing content (except undergarments and enveloping cover on non-human form).   [Phillips and Smith]

Affect and Emotional Needs

Agitation potential:

C.Y blend; CF.Y blend (Beck and Molish); M.Y blend. (Beck III)

Appropriate emotional responsivity:

Pleasantly toned color comments. (Phillips and Smith)

Appropriate responsivity to emotionally provocative stimuli from the environment:

R VIII, IX, X greater than 30–40%. (Klopfer-Developments I)

Avoidance of conscious awareness of affect:

Exclusive form-determined R. (Schafer-Rorschach)

Blandness:

Absence of shading; low P with low sum color. (Schafer-Clinical Application)

Cheerful emotional tone (cheerful emotional mood):

Affectionate gestures; candy and ice cream; carnival; children; children bundled up; children's garments; circus; clown; cradle; dancing; dragons; elves; embrace; fireworks; frolic; increment of children's storybook characters and figures; kissing; leggings; ogre; snuggling; toy; wizard content. (Schafer-Rorschach)

Constrained emotional tone:

Anemometer content; governor on steam engine content; shell content. (Schafer-Rorschach)

Control of emotions without involvement; impersonal, matter-of-fact approach:

High F%, form good. (Klopfer-Davidson)

Cyclic mood swings:

Emphasis on space or color as light, reacted to positively, while shading is reacted to negatively. (Schafer-Rorschach)

Decrement of emotional responsivity:

Sum color less than three. (Klopfer-Davidson)

Denial of affect:	Increment Dd. (Schafer-Rorschach)
Dependency needs (desire for dependency):	Complimentary remarks about cards; religion content (Phillips and Smith); food content (Klopfer-Davidson); lamb content (Schafer-Rorschach); puppy. (Beck and Molish)
Dependency needs possibly:	Household content. (Beck III)
Depressed or dysphoric mood:	Mourning content. (Schafer-Rorschach)
Desire for nurturance and support:	Outstretched hands on H. (Phillips and Smith)
Despair:	YF-. (Beck and Molish)
Detached emotional tone (emotional detachment):	Dd (edge details) (Phillips and Smith); Ice, iceberg content; nature content. (Schafer-Rorschach)
Direct reflection of feeling tone, dysphoric or euphoric:	Abstraction content. (Klopfer-Davidson).
Discouragement:	Decrement S, increment of A and shading (Beck III); remarks suggesting feeling of resignation over inability to produce response or further responses. (Phillips and Smith)
Dysphoric mood:	FY (Phillips and Smith);M.Y (Beck III); map content. (Phillips and Smith)
Dysphoric mood, probably expressed through fantasy:	FY.M. (Beck III)
Elation potential:	Increment F+ color with positively toned affective comments. (Beck III)
Emotional turmoil:	Chaos; high wind; lightning; storm clouds; explosion and fire; threatening or violent weather; thunderstorm; volcano. (Schafer-Rorschach)

Emphasis on emotional control:	Enclosing, geometrically exact and regulatory objects. (Schafer-Rorschach)
Euphoria:	Animal content decrement. (Phillips and Smith)
Exciting or gratifying fantasy:	Color. M. (Beck III)
Expansive tendency:	Increment color and M. (Rapaport)
Feeling of dejection and deprivation of affection:	Turkey content. (Phillips and Smith)
Feeling of rejection with dysphoric affect preoccupation:	TF, VF, YF. (Beck and Molish)
Felt weakness with need for guidance and support:	Supporting objects. (Schafer-Rorschach)
Flat affect:	No color associations. (Beck III)
Good emotional control:	FC on IX. (Rapaport)
Hypersensitivity:	CF. (Beck and Molish)
Hypomanic tendency:	Abstractions, confabulation, decrement A, increment W, C, CF, Dd, S, shading, self-reference. (Schafer-Rorschach)
Hysteric affect:	Repulsion expressed to blot appearance. (Phillips and Smith)
Inadequate emotional control:	C + CF greater than FC; CF. (Klopfer-Davidson)
In adults impairment of emotional control:	FC-. (Klopfer-Developments I)
Inappropriate affect:	C and CF with low affective ratio (Beck III); color greater than M (Rapaport); pure C. (Schafer-Clinical Application)
Inappropriateness of affect and behavior rather than systematized delusions:	Absence of M, emphasis on pure C, low F+. (Schafer-Clinical Application)
Infantile need for nurturance and physical contact:	T. (Klopfer-Davidson)
Intellectualization of affect:	Color description and color naming. (Klopfer-Davidson)

Lability (emotional lability):

Botany or nature CF; hysterical features with low F+; perceiving cards as "evil" or "revolting"; loss of distance from percepts (Schafer-Rorschach); C and CF with low affective ratio; increment CF; F-, low-form color, rapid card turning, rapid speech, restlessness (Beck III); increment C, CF. (Beck and Molish)

Lack of emotional spontaneity:

F + FT + FV greater than 75%. (Klopfer-Davidson)

Lack of flexibility or modulation of emotional tone:

Only one type of color-determinant (C, CF, FC). [Beck and Molish]

Manic tendency:

Color abstractions; intense verbalized negative or positive reactions to color (Beck III); constant speech; emphasis on C and CF. (Beck and Molish)

Masochism with defeatist tendency and oppressive feeling:

Yoke content. (Schafer-Rorschach)

May suggest flattened affect tendency:

Introversive orientation with absence of color shock and increment of FY shading. (Klopfer-Developments I)

Mood of well-being:

Butterfly (nonpopular). (Phillips and Smith)

Need for affection:

FT. (Beck and Molish)

Need for dependent compliance:

FT plus color. (Klopfer Developments I)

Need for guidance and support:

Guiding beams (beacon, lighthouse). [Schafer-Rorschach]

Need for help and protection:

Asking for confirmation of adequacy of the response and for reassurance. (Schafer-Rorschach)

Need for innocence:

Cradle, lamb, sleeping infant. (Schafer-Rorschach)

Negative feelings:

Cut content. (Schafer-Rorschach)

Neurotic affect:

Color shock on Card IX. (Klopfer-Developments I)

Nostalgia for childhood dependency state:	Cut content; dragon content; elephant content; rabbit content; seahorse. (Phillips and Smith)
Nurturance needs:	Area D11 of Card VII as house. (Klopfer-Davidson)
Oppressive feeling:	Animal held down; ox content. (Schafer-Rorschach)
Oppressive painful anticipation of unpleasantness:	Bat content (in nonpopular area). [Phillips and Smith]
Overcontrol:	Increment FC. (Klopfer-Developments I)
Overcontrolled affect:	Color denial, negative reaction to color. (Beck and Molish)
Overcontrolled affect with dislike of intense emotion:	Smooth texture. (Phillips and Smith)
Painful affect:	Blends; M.Y blend (Beck III); C.Y blend; low-form color with low-form shading in blend response. (Beck and Molish)
Passive-dependency:	Neonate or small animals. (Beck III)
Passive-submissive needs that may be denied:	Celebrated and powerful persons. (Schafer-Rorschach)
Pleasantly toned affect, if not countered by negative determinants:	Botany, feminine clothing, nature content. (Beck and Molish)
Potential for affective response:	Low number color associations; high affective ratio. (Beck III)
Potential for agitation state (potential for excitement states):	C, CF with shading (Beck III); low-form color with low-form shading in blend response (Beck and Molish); pure C (with low A and F%). [Schafer-Clinical Application]
Potential for agitation state possibly:	Blends. (Beck III)
Potential for panic state:	Pure C with low A and F%. (Schafer-Clinical Application)
Potential for bizarre panic state:	Shading increment, schizophrenic tendency. (Schafer-Clinical Application)

Potential possibly for panic state:	Oral threat animal content, as crocodiles, wolves. (Beck and Molish)
Rejection of affective experience:	Color rejection. (Beck III)
Resignation:	YF-. (Beck and Molish)
Responsivity or potential for responsivity:	Percent R VIII, IX, X greater than 10. (Klopfer Developments I)
Sadness, unhappy emotional tone:	Mourning content; ruins content; tears content. (Schafer-Rorschach)
Sensitivity:	FT; FT response to popular animal, Card II (Klopfer-Developments I); FT optimal (Phillips and Smith); tender descriptions. (Schafer-Clinical Application)
Submissive feelings:	Bowing, cowering, listening H. (Klopfer-Davidson)
Suicidal tendency possibly, especially in intelligent persons who display painful affect:	High-places content. (Beck and Molish)
Very painful affect:	Color with shading. (Beck III)
Volatility:	Affective ratio or percent color of about 80 or more (Beck III); chaos content; explosion content; fire content; high-wind content; lightning content; storm clouds; thunderstorm content; volcano content. (Schafer-Rorschach)
Weakness with need for guidance and support:	Beacon content; cane content; crutch content; handles content; lighthouse content. (Schafer-Rorschach)

Alternative or Concurrent Behavior

Aggression, which may either take the passive form of somatization or be expressed by temper tantrums:	Blood content. (Rapaport)
Alcoholism and schizophrenia:	Anatomy content, low F+ combination. (Beck and Molish)

Anxiety plus depression:	F+ approaching 100%. (Phillips and Smith)
Assertive or oppositional tendency:	Increment space. (Klopfer-Developments I)
Conflict between activity and passivity:	Static M. (Phillips and Smith)
Conflict between compliance and negativistic hostility:	Increment FC plus space responses. (Schafer-Rorschach)
Critical, possibly perfectionistic subject:	Increment Wx. (Klopfer-Developments I)
Dependency needs countered by negativism:	Failure to turn card after asking permission. (Phillips and Smith)
Dependency needs with inferiority feelings:	Hills content. (Phillips and Smith)
Dependency needs or need for innocence:	Sleeping infant. (Schafer-Rorschach)
Dependency needs or need for reassurance:	Cradle content. (Schafer-Rorschach)
Destructiveness; or inhibition:	No color. (Phillips and Smith)
Dysphoric and painful affect:	Shading shock. (Beck III)
Feared or wished-for attitude or prevailing mood with anxiety:	Fabulization. (Phillips and Smith)
Feeling of hopelessness and ineffectuality:	Edging, shock, Card IV. (Phillips and Smith)
Feeling of inadequacy with facade of assurance and confidence:	Magnified microscopic life-form content. (Schafer-Rorschach)
Ideas of reference or influence:	Eyes content. (Phillips and Smith)
Indifference (except when indifference is due to resistiveness):	Lackadaisical comments on mild disparity between R and blot outlines. (Phillips and Smith)
Inhibition of action for fear of punishment alternating with acting out of hostility:	Complimentary remarks about card followed by disparaging comments. (Phillips and Smith)
Ingratiation followed by provocation:	Complimentary remarks about card followed by disparaging comments. (Phillips and Smith)

Inhibition; or querulousness:

Lack of capacity for affection or rejection of need for it:

Lack of initiative; or possible passivity:

Malingering or resistiveness·

Manifest and social anxiety:

Marked anxiety or impetuosity:

Masochism possibly, or sadism:

May be creative, sensitive, spontaneous subject, or one who tends to overpersonalize reactions:

May be determination or externalized hostility:

May represent negativism, obstinacy, or rebelliousness in conjunction with obsessive-compulsive meticulousness:

Narcissism or somatization tendency:

Obsequiousness in conjunction with verbal expression of hostility:

Oppressive and morbid self-preoccupation, with depressive rumination, irritability, and passivity:

Overdeferentiality with indirect expression of hostility for fear of punishment:

Paranoid or combined paranoid-phobic tendency:

Passive-aggressive ("oral-aggressive") or denial of passive-aggressive trends:

Passive-aggressive ("oral-aggressive") or passive-receptive trend:

No color. (Phillips and Smith)

Avoidance of shading. (Klopfer-Davidson)

No space responses. (Beck and Molish)

Statement that blots do not suggest a response. (Phillips and Smith)

M greater than H. (Phillips and Smith)

C, CF, T, TF. (Schafer-Rorschach)

Cannibal content; eagle's beak; tusks content; vulture content. (Klopfer-Davidson)

Low F+ with optimal color, M, shading. (Klopfer-Davidson)

Increment space. (Beck III)

Increment space in setting of overconscientious perfectionism. (Schafer-Rorschach)

Figures exercising. (Schafer-Rorschach)

Rough texture. (Phillips and Smith)

Fabulization. (Phillips and Smith)

Rough texture. (Phillips and Smith)

"Sinister" percepts. (Schafer-Rorschach)

Mosquito content. (Schafer-Rorschach)

Beggar content. (Schafer-Rorschach)

Passive-compliance with obsessive-compulsive features:	Inquiry as to what to do with card after responding to it. (Phillips and Smith)
Passive-submissive, or defense against passive-submissive needs:	Crown or other kingly paraphernalia content; Franklin or Teddy Roosevelt content; general content; king content; lumberjack content; Hercules content; muscular figures; Napoleon content; Norseman content; truck driver content; warrior content. (Schafer-Rorschach)
Passive-submissive or intellectual defense against passive-submissive needs:	Buddha content; Christ content; Einstein content; Lincoln content; Shakespeare content; Socrates content; statesmen and wise men. (Schafer-Rorschach)
Regression and schizophrenia if F−:	Astronomy content. (Phillips and Smith)
Sadism, possible masochism:	Claws content; lions content; wild boar; wolf content. (Schafer-Rorschach)
Sadomasochistic orientation:	Automaton content. (Schafer-Rorschach)
Superego conflict with both guilt and overt hostility:	Stain content. (Schafer-Rorschach)
Symbolizes innocent attitudes possibly, or reaction-formation as defense against hostile impulses:	Angel content. (Schafer-Rorschach)
With aggressive animal or human content, may represent possible paranoid tendency or a displacement defense:	Decrement F+, high Z score, increment S, paranoid content themes. (Beck III)

Aspiration

Ambition:	Architecture content (Rapaport); good form, W above expectancy. (Phillips and Smith)
Ambition for accomplishment with potential for it:	W:M ratio 2:1. (Klopfer-Davidson)

Aspiration below potential capacity:	W less than two times M. (Klopfer-Developments I)
Aspiration felt to be unobtainable:	Vista—distances and heights. (Beck and Molish)
Defense against sadomasochism with rejection of adult role:	Brassiere content; Breastplate content. (Schafer-Rorschach)
Dependency, with indifference to adult role and poor prognosis:	Food content. (Phillips and Smith)
Grandiose ambition and compensatory emphasis on intellectual achievement possibly:	F + W. (Schafer-Rorschach)
High level of aspiration:	Bridge content. (Phillips and Smith)
Lack of long-range goals:	CF dominance; precision alternatives with first rejected for second; recreation content; response time 5″ (Phillips and Smith); "floating" percepts (clouds, etc.) [Schafer-Rorschach]; FM greater than two times M, if CF greater than FC. (Klopfer-Davidson)
Lack of middle class aspirations:	Incorrect grammar. (Phillips and Smith)
Lack of spontaneity:	Machines, precision maneuvers, statue. (Schafer-Rorschach)
Limited aspiration:	Emphasis on D. (Phillips and Smith)
Little drive for achievement, limited ambition:	Mediocre W, underemphasis on W. (Beck and Molish)
Long-range goals:	M+. (Phillips and Smith)
Maturity and capacity to work for long-range goals:	M greater than 2 exceeds FM, which is greater than zero. (Klopfer-Davidson)
May indicate lack of motivation for achievement:	Increment of A content. (Beck and Molish)
Motivation for long-range goals:	M greater than FM, FM at least half of M. (Klopfer-Developments I)

Realistic aspiration with minimum 3M, 6W:

W:M ratio 2:1. (Klopfer-Developments I)

Rejection of adult role:

Alice in Wonderland content; animals devouring other animals or persons; animals or persons arguing, spitting, sticking tongues out, yelling; Atlas content; baby crocodiles; biting animals; baker content; big-belly content; bird on nest content; bone or chicken neck with the meat removed; bunny content; cannibal content; carcass content; chicks with open beaks; children-bundled-up content; children content; children's garment content; Christmas stocking; Christmas tree; circus content; claws content; cornucopia content; cow content; coyote content; crab content (other than popular D1, D7, and D8 of Card X); cradle content; crocodile content; decanter content; dentist's tools; dragon content; eagle's beak; elves content; emaciated animal detail; emaciated cow head; emaciated face; embryo, fetus; false teeth content; fangs content; fat-bellied devils; fat-cheeked pussy cat; fat-person content; feeding animals; fighting animals; figures kissing; fireworks content; frying pan content; good-fairy content; hands raised in supplication; ice cream content; increment children's storybook characters and figures; infant carnivorous animals; jaws content; leggings content; lion content; lips content; little demons; lizard content; horseshoe content; man weighted down by pack; mice tearing down a house; mother bird with worm; mother hen content; mouthless or toothless face; mule content;

navel content; nipples content; nurse content; nursing lamb content; ogre content; partially consumed animals and objects, person-eating content; person-praying content; pig content; pit content; preying animals; protective angel, pursuing animals; Santa Claus content; shark content; skin eaten away by bugs; skull of steer in desert; Snow White content; spider-web content; stomach content; syrup jar; table-setting content; tapeworm content; teeth content; throat content; tiger content; tiny lions; tomato worm content; tusks content; umbilical content; vampire content; waiter content; wild boar content; wishbone content, other than D3 on X; wizard content; wolf content; woman with enveloping cloak.
(Schafer-Rorschach)

Unrealistic ambition:

Increment W; mediocre but not vague form or increment of F– (Klopfer-Developments I); W:M ratio 3:1 (Phillips and Smith); W greater than two times M.   (Klopfer-Davidson; Klopfer-Developments I; Rapaport)

Attitude

Aggressive attitudes:

Disparagement of Rorschach and test figures. (Toubin, Beck and Molish)

Authoritarian attitude (authoritarian orientation):

Automaton content; elevated or low social status symbols; Prussian content; symbols of imprisonment; symbols of rebellion and revolution.
(Schafer-Rorschach)

Authoritarian attitude (authoritarian orientation; concern with authority and power):

Admiral content; authoritative, supernatural, or threatening figures; crest content; crown and other kingly paraphernalia; fierce or huge figure; general content; God content; Jehovah content; king content; Ku Klux Klan figures; Napoleon content; person addressing multitude; person giving orders; policeman content; queen content; ragged or torn objects; robot content; seal of state; scepter content; throne content. (Schafer-Rorschach)

Authoritarian attitude (authoritarian orientation), with conformity, rigidity, tension:

No turning. (Phillips and Smith)

Authoritarian attitude (authoritarian orientation), with felt inferior social status:

Peasant content. (Schafer-Rorschach)

Authoritarian attitude (authoritarian orientation), with felt inferior social status and submission:

Servant content. (Schafer-Rorschach)

Authoritarian attitude (authoritarian orientation), with impersonal relationships and sadomasochistic orientation:

Bowed, debased, powerless, slovenly, subjugated persons; performing animals and pets. (Schafer-Rorschach)

Authoritarian attitude (authoritarian orientation), with impersonal and sadomasochistic relationships and sadistic impulses:

Authoritative, savage, threatening figures. (Schafer-Rorschach)

Authoritarian attitude (authoritarian orientation), with inadequacy:

Crushed or squashed figure. (Schafer-Rorschach)

Authoritarian attitude (authoritarian orientation), with negative attitudes and submission:

Trained seal. (Schafer-Rorschach)

Authoritarian attitude (authoritarian orientation), with rebelliousness:

American Indian content; broken chains content; Communist emblem content; Confederate flag content; cracked yoke; devil content; gangster content; Liberty Bell; Loki content; person sticking tongue out. (Schafer-Rorschach)

Authoritarian attitude (authoritarian orientation) with submission:

Chains content; chess pawn content; clipped French poodle content;

	kneeling position content; marionette content; parrot content; prison bars content; trained monkey content; yoke content. (Schafer-Rorschach)
Conventionality (conformity, over-conformity, overconventionality):	A greater than 50%; enumeration of parts; FC; further inquiries about turning card after permission is given; missing part content; nonblatant religious Human content (priest, etc.); texture (FT) [Phillips and Smith]; FC (Schafer-Rorschach); P (Phillips and Smith; Rapaport); increment P (Anderson-Beck; Beck and Molish; Beck III; Klopfer-Davidson; Klopfer-Developments I); increment P (8+). (Klopfer-Davidson)
Criticality:	(A + H) less than ½ (Ad + Hd) [Klopfer-Davidson]; excluding parts of popular, Card I; (H); Hd; increment Dd; side D profile, Card I. (Klopfer-Developments I)
Defensive attitudes:	Protected animals like porcupine; protective clothing, devices, and structures; sheltering terrain. (Schafer-Rorschach)
Demanding attitude:	Animals devouring other animals or persons; animals or people arguing, spitting, sticking tongues out; yelling, arguing, and deriding animals or people; Atlas content; beggar content; biting animals; brassiere content; breastplate content; burdened animals and people; camel content; cannibal content; carcass content; carnivorous animals and insects; clawing animals; claws content; cloaked woman; coyote content; crab content other than popular D1, D7, and D8 of Card X; crocodile content; dentist's tools; Dracula; eagle's beak; emaciated face;

emaciated or tattered figures (beggar, scarecrow); false teeth; flat- or small-bosomed woman; fangs content; feeding animals; fighting animals; jaws content; lion content; man-weighted-down-by-pack content; mosquito content; mouthless or toothless face; mule content; ox content; person-sticking-tongue-out content; pit content; plant-devouring-animals content; preying-animals content; pursuing-animals content; scarecrow content; shark content; skull-of-steer-in-desert content; spider content; spider web; tapeworm content; tattered figures; teeth content; tiger content; tomato worm content; trap content; tusks content; vampire content; vise content; vulture content; wasteland content; wild boar content; witch content; wolf content; woman with enveloping cloak (Schafer-Rorschach); C + CF greater than FC; pure C (more than one). [Phillips and Smith]

Demanding querulousness: — Complaining about demands of test or time it takes; decline of R as test continues. (Schafer-Rorschach)

Derisive attitudes: — Monkey content. (Phillips and Smith)

Derogatory attitudes possibly: — "Clowns," Card II. (Klopfer-Developments I)

Exacting attitudes: — (A + H) less than ½ (Ad + Hd). (Klopfer-Davidson)

Excessive concern with the proprieties possibly: — Increment P. (Beck and Molish)

Formality: — Exclusive FC. (Phillips and Smith)

Hostility with overcriticality: — Decrement A + H, increment Ad and Hd. (Klopfer-Developments I)

Hypercriticality possibly: — Rejection of cards, rejection of response after verbalized. (Schafer-Rorschach)

Negative attitudes (general negativistic attitudes):	Alligators content; crocodile content; derogatory remarks about cards; fox content; immediate consistent turning, usually with R given to upright position; lizard content; rat content; wolf content (Phillips and Smith); awkward or missing wings on birds content; badly baked cookie content; badly tied bow tie content; blind or missing eyes content; body without backbone content; chains content; chess pawn content; clipped French poodle; crudely skinned animal; crushed or squashed figures; dangling legs content; dead branch content; drooping arms content; emaciated face; hands raised in supplication content; hut content; kneeling position content; marionette content; mice barely hanging on; parrot content; peasant content; pliers content; prison bars content; ragged or torn clothes content; robot content; servant content; skull of steer in desert content; smeared slide; straw man; trained monkey content; tree stump content; wasteland content; yoke content. (Schafer-Rorschach)
Obstinacy (stubbornness):	Color greater than M, M greater than average (Phillips and Smith); mule content (Schafer-Rorschach); figure ground reversal space (Beck III; Klopfer-Davidson); space (Anderson-Beck); space with increment color. (Rapaport)
Pomposity, perhaps to compensate for feeling of inadequacy:	Use of editorial "we." (Schafer-Rorschach)
Regressive attitude:	M in A. (Phillips and Smith)
Self-righteous attitude:	Criticism of cards. (Schafer-Rorschach)

Submissive attitude toward authority: Emblem content. (Klopfer-
Developments I)

Unconventional attitudes (indifference   Absence of popular as first response,
to conventions):   Card I (Phillips and Smith); decrement
of populars. (Anderson-Beck)

Cognitive Functions

Ability to concentrate, clarity of   Form accuracy. (Rorschach-
associative processes, length of   *Psychodiagnostics*)
attention span:

Abstraction: Increment F + W. (Rapaport)

Apperceptive type: Location response—use of the whole
blot (W), of a large usual detail (D),
or of a small unusual detail (Dd).
(Rorschach-*Psychodiagnostics*)

Attention to detail with reluctance   Emphasis on D and Dd. (Klopfer-
to generalize: Davidson)

Concreteness (concretism):   Increment D (Beck III); W greater
than two times M. (Rapaport)

Degree of stereotypy: Percentage of animal responses.
(Rorschach-*Psychodiagnostics*)

Generalization from integration   Optimum W. (Rapaport)
of data:

Generalization with appropriate   D and W optimum. (Klopfer-
attention to details: Davidson)

Intellectual control: F+. (Phillips and Smith)

Lack of creativity and imagination: Decrement M, increment R.
(Beck III)

Logical discipline of thinking: Sequence of location responses.
(Rorschach-*Psychodiagnosis*)

Overgeneralization (tendency to   Increment DW or vague W (Rapaport);
jump to conclusions):   increment W; mediocre but not
vague form or increment of F− (Klopfer-Developments I); overemphasis on
W. (Klopfer-Davidson)

Stereotypy: Animal content (Phillips and Smith);
A greater than 50% (Klopfer-Davidson);

geography content; increment A, At or perseveration of vague form; increment P; landscape content; vague form (Rapaport); high A% (Phillips and Smith; Rapaport); stereotyped phrases. (Beck III)

Contraindications

Contraindicates acting out:

Abstraction content; bony anatomy content; cool color preference; fabulization; form dominance; M increment; nonchildren's-literature H; shading (Phillips and Smith); decrement color, increment S; increment nonabstract F + Fm. (Klopfer-Developments I)

Contraindicates assaultiveness:

Abstraction content; anatomy content; blocked or passive M; blood content; control by external forces; emphasis on Hd limbs or projections; FC; Fm responses; part body M; presence of FC; shading; stop motion H.
(Phillips and Smith)

Contraindicates character disorder:

Conservative responses.
(Schafer-Clinical Application)

Contraindicates chronic schizophrenia:

Increment of animal content.
(Rapaport)

Contraindicates depressive trend:

Pure C (more than one) [Phillips and Smith] ; increment M. (Rapaport)

Contraindicates destructiveness:

Hd limbs (arms and legs) content.
(Phillips and Smith)

Contraindicates hysteria as primary process:

Increment R. (Beck and Molish)

Contraindicates hysteric trends:

Increment M. (Rapaport)

Contraindicates immaturity:

Abstraction content; M in abstraction.
(Phillips and Smith)

Contraindicates impulsive acting out:

FY. (Phillips and Smith)

Contraindicates inadequacy:

Abstraction content.   (Phillips and Smith)

Contraindicates malingering:

Stated inability to produce a response. (Phillips and Smith)

Contraindicates manic state:

Emphasis on introversive (M) in experience balance. (Beck and Molish)

Contraindicates neurasthenic trend:

Increment M. (Rapaport)

Contraindicates neurotic state:

Indifference to shading. (Klopfer-Developments I)

Contraindicates obsessive-compulsive trend:

Decrement M. (Rapaport)

Contraindicates paranoid trend:

Increment color; increment M. (Rapaport)

Contraindicates antisocial behavior ("psychopathy"):

M in abstraction. (Phillips and Smith)

Contraindicates psychosis:

Increment nonabstract F + Fm. (Klopfer-Developments I)

Contraindicates retardation:

High F+. (Beck and Molish)

Contraindicates shyness:

M in abstraction. (Phillips and Smith)

Contraindicates tension:

M in abstraction. (Phillips and Smith)

Passive-aggressive ("oral-aggressive") personality, but otherwise contraindicates acting out and assaultiveness:

Visceral anatomy content (especially on Cards I, VIII, IX and X). [Phillips and Smith]

Sadistic impulses, but acting out is contraindicated:

Blood content. (Phillips and Smith)

Defenses

Anxiety at least partially bound by characterologic defenses:

Evidence of emotional disturbance without color shock. (Beck and Molish)

Anxiety over frustrated need for affection with intellectualization; FY with more effective intellectualization:

FY, YF, Y. (Klopfer-Davidson)

Autism (autistic or reality-alienated fantasy):

M in Dd (Phillips and Smith); M in form-minus animal movement (FM-) [Beck and Molish]; M-. (Beck III)

Autism, daydreaming, excessive immersion in fantasy:

Excessive R total for VIII, IX, X, as compared to other cards. (Beck and Molish)

Autism possibly:	Exceptionally low animal content. (Beck III)
Autism or self-absorption:	Self-references. (Schafer-Rorschach)
Avoidance (avoidance tendency):	Animal detail content (Ad); color naming; Hd content; perplexity (Beck and Molish); card rejection; delayed reaction time; short total time for card (Schafer-Rorschach); Dd (edge details) [Klopfer-Developments I] ; rejections (Beck III); response time 40″ or more. (Phillips and Smith)
Avoidance of direct confrontation of problems:	Dd or edge details. (Klopfer-Davidson)
Avoidance of insight and self-analysis:	Statement that blots do not suggest a response. (Phillips and Smith)
Avoidance in presence of stimuli like that suggested by the card rejected:	Rejection without evidence of guardedness. (Schafer-Rorschach)
Blocking:	Bony anatomy content; increment anatomy content; long reaction time (Rapaport); experience balance of 0:0; slow response time (Beck and Molish); very slow response; very slow time for first response. (Beck III)
Caution:	Dd M; response time 40″ or more (Phillips and Smith); diminutive, passive, or plodding animals. (Schafer-Rorschach)
Caution with alertness:	Eyes content. (Beck III)
Caution although impulsive acts may be sporadically expressed:	High F+%, increment M, low color. (Schafer-Rorschach)
Caution in presence of emotionally provocative situations:	Single response on X. (Schafer-Clinical Application)
Compensatory emphasis on intellectual attainment:	Neural anatomy content. (Phillips and Smith)
Compensation for feelings of inadequacy possibly:	Increment R, narrow content. (Beck III)

Conflict between reaction-formation against hostility and narcissistic rebellious impulses, with defenses inadequate to contain the negativistic tendency:

Increment Dd and F–. (Schafer-Rorschach)

Concealment of the self:

Mask content. (Klopfer-Davidson)

Conformity:

"Bending over" content. (Phillips and Smith)

Constriction:

Ambiequal experience balance; no more than one color and M; H greater than Hd (Beck and Molish); decrement color, M, shading, high F% (50–80) (Klopfer-Davidson); decrement M and FM; form-plus if greater than 50% (Klopfer-Developments I); extended F+ greater than 90%; increment F+; increment P; little island content (Schafer-Rorschach); increment F+%; narrow experience balance (Rapaport); increment qualification, precision alternatives, stereotyped phrases, symmetry; low color and M in experience balance (coarctate experience balance); no turning. (Beck III)

Constriction with feeling of isolation and loneliness:

Wasteland content. (Schafer-Rorschach)

Constriction of neurotic kind:

F + FT + FV greater than 75%. (Klopfer-Davidson)

Constriction of pathological degree:

F% greater than 80, good form. (Klopfer-Davidson)

Constriction produced by anxiety:

Hd content. (Beck III)

Conversion:

Hysterical features with anatomical content. (Schafer-Clinical Application)

Counterphobic resistance to passive-submissive needs:

"Ancient tribal mask that once was frightening"; comic book monster; "ridiculous ghost" content; toy gorilla. (Schafer-Rorschach)

Decompensating obsessive-compulsive defense system possibly:

Anal percepts; decrement F+; "destructive" remarks about cards ("if you chop it off here," etc.); increment anxious, hostile imagery; color, shading. (Schafer-Rorschach)

Defense against passive-submissive needs:

Facetiousness, negativistic reaction to testing. (Schafer-Rorschach)

Defense against sadomasochistic tendency:

Armor content; camouflage content; fortress content; helmet content; hip guards; moat content; porcupine content; shell content; shoulder pads content; thicket content; turrets content; valley content; visor content. (Schafer-Rorschach)

Defense against sadomasochistic or paranoid tendency:

Shield content. (Schafer-Rorschach)

Defenses and habits stereotyped:

Rigid sequence, increment of D. (Beck III)

Defenses and reality testing inadequate:

Anxiety or disgust reactions with arbitrary or diffuse form. (Schafer-Rorschach)

Defense system adequate even if perhaps mildly unstable:

Absence of popular as initial response, inadequate form but subsequent response F+ and/or no manifest anxiety clinically observable and no schizophrenic tendency. (Schafer-Rorschach)

Defense system against conflict areas ineffective and rigid:

Determinants appearing only in minus forms. (Klopfer-Developments I)

Defense system effective:

Absence of excessive verbiage, and of anxiety and of prolonged doubting in an obsessive-compulsive setting, if evidence of psychosis is not present. (Schafer-Rorschach)

Defense system relatively successful:

Decrement shading and sum color; dominance FC over CF; increment F+%. (Schafer-Rorschach)

Defense system stable:

Positive emotional tone (humor, responsivity, relative freedom from manifest anxiety) [Phillips and Smith];

extended F+ 80–90%; sincerely accepting or positive attitude toward Rorschach determinants; expression of pleasure relative to color or the nature of the task. (Schafer-Rorschach)

Defense system stable (or rigid):

Sincerely accepting or positive attitude toward Rorschach determinants; expression of pleasure relative to color or the nature of the task.
(Schafer-Rorschach)

Defense system unstable:

Extended F+ below 80%; increment space; marked increment M to minimum color, as ten M to zero sum color; marked increment of W (more than 20); negation or withdrawal of a response—negative attitude toward test elements or toward examiner; negative emotional tone (lack of appropriate humor and cooperation); presence of moderate to severe anxiety; unresponsiveness.
(Schafer-Rorschach)

Defense system unstable possibly:

Absence of popular as initial response, inadequate form; forgetting percepts. (Schafer-Rorschach)

Defense system weak and ineffective:

Perceptual vagueness. (Schafer-Rorschach)

Delayed response:

Diminutive, passive, or plodding animals; mask. (Schafer-Rorschach)

Denial:

Ingratiation; minimizing of negative or painful reaction to life experiences and test stimuli; Pollyanna attitudes; long reaction time followed by references on chromatic cards to meaninglessness of color. (Schafer-Rorschach)

Denial of anxiety:

Avoidance of shading or emphasis only on light rather than heavy shading. (Schafer-Rorschach)

Denial of anxiety and depression possibly; oppositional trend may also be present:	Response to inner space (Ds 5) of Card II, with black area (D6) as background. (Schafer-Rorschach)
Denial of anxiety possibly:	Shading denial. (Schafer-Rorschach)
Denial of guilt as a defense (along with innocence) against superego anxiety:	Alice in Wonderland content; angel content; bunny content; cathedral content; cherub content; good fairy; halo; Jesus content; lamb content; Madonna content; monk content; nun content; saint content; Snow White content; snow-white buttocks content. (Schafer-Rorschach)
Denial of hostility:	Blood content followed by over-deferential attitude toward the examiner; making ferocious animals cartoon characters (Schafer-Rorschach); nun content; saint content; Snow White content; snow-white buttocks content. (Schafer-Rorschach)
Denial, including anxiety denial:	Increased productivity on cards following that which elicits color shock. (Beck and Molish)
Denial of orality possibly:	Missing or small mouth comments. (Schafer-Rorschach)
Denial of passive-aggressive ("oral-aggressive") trend:	Artificial or missing biting and punching surfaces (false teeth, toothless faces); little devouring or attacking animals (minature dragons, mosquitoes). [Schafer-Rorschach]
Denial of passive-submissive needs possibly:	Belittled frightening animals (comic book animals); heroic leaders and persons; powerful animals or figures. (Schafer-Rorschach)
Denial possibly:	Increment euphorically toned associations; making large objects small (as "twig") for Card III, D5 area more often seen as a "tree branch"; ostrich content. (Schafer-Rorschach)

Denial possibly; lack of insight into emotional difficulties:	No FM with evident emotional conflict. (Klopfer-Davidson)
Denial or repression of dependency:	FT + FV less than ¼ F. (Klopfer-Davidson)
Denial or repression of tendency the object represents:	Making a percept a drawing, as a caricature, or making it lifeless, as a preserved or museum specimen. (Schafer-Rorschach)
Denial of tendency or threat the association implies:	Negative form responses; negative percepts ("It's not a ___"). (Schafer-Rorschach)
Depressive trend that is defended against:	Color naming, cool colors. (Beck and Molish)
Destructive impulses expressed by excessive defensive constriction and constraint:	Edging, shock (men more than women), Card II. (Phillips and Smith)
Displacement:	Aggressive A; decrement F+; increment S; high Z score; H with paranoid content themes; Hd content. (Beck III)
Doubt (doubting tendency):	Ambiequal experience balance, S increment (Beck III); H, Hd content; (H) content; turning, few or no responses with card turned (Klopfer-Developments I); long reaction time; space with increment Dd, P, M (Rapaport); space in obsessive-compulsive protocol. (Beck and Molish)
Effort to compensate for feelings of inadequacy:	Increment FV with increment R. (Beck III)
Elusiveness:	Texture (FT). (Phillips and Smith)
Escapist or wish-fulfilling fantasy:	Decrement W, increment M. (Klopfer-Developments I)
Evasion:	Art content; clouds content; Dd; Dd (edge details); map content; "you" forms (Phillips and Smith); edge interpretations. (Rapaport)

Evasion of insight or issues with displacement:

Increment Dd. (Beck III)

Fairly effective counterphobic defenses:

More than one response to cards, quick response to disturbing card areas. (Schafer-Rorschach)

Fantasy activity:

M. (Beck and Molish)

Feeling of inadequacy or insecurity that may be denied or unconscious:

Card III popular H as minority group members. (Klopfer-Developments I)

Felt emotional instability guarded against by defense mechanisms:

"Base" percept. (Schafer-Rorschach)

Guardedness:

Abstraction content; Hd content; increment P (Rapaport); A increment; clouds content; elaboration below expectancy; F% above expectancy; F+% above expectancy; high A%; R below expectancy; excessive rejections; reduction of M; reduction of R; smiling at examiner; stereotyped popular response imitiating Rorschach (Phillips and Smith); increment of D, rigid sequence; increment F+ (Beck III); map content (Klopfer-Davidson); rejections. (Schafer-Rorschach)

Guardedness possibly:

Increment FC. (Schafer-Rorschach)

Hostile impulses defended against by avoidance, resentful passive-compliance, or withdrawal:

Blood content followed by evasion. (Schafer-Rorschach)

Ideational tendency:

Dd increment; M increment or M without color (Schafer-Clinical Application); Dd perseveration; edge details; esoteric phrases and terms; face content; FY; looking at back of cards; pedantry. (Phillips and Smith)

Immature, wish-fulfilling fantasy:

(H) M. (Klopfer-Developments I)

Impulsivity followed by attempt at repressive control:

CF response followed by form-determined response. (Klopfer-Developments I)

Indecision:

Doubt expressed about adequacy of a percept; precision alternatives (Phillips and Smith); flexor stance (Beck III): space in obsessive-compulsive protocol. (Beck and Molish)

Infantile or repressive behavior:

Egg, nest content, center upper D, Card VI. (Klopfer-Developments I)

Inhibition:

Abstraction content; form-determined content; increment of animal content; increment F%; increment rejection; narrow experience balance; W:D ratio 1:2 (Rapaport); achromatic to chromatic greater than 2:1; additional FM and M, increment F; color responses less than non–color responses; shading twice number of color responses (Klopfer-Developments I); constricted experience balance; delayed reaction time; discrepancy between good intelligence and low R; excessive FC; high F+; low CF; single response to X (Schafer-Clinical Application); decrement color (Rapaport; Klopfer-Davidson); enumeration of parts; FY minus color; missing parts comment; reduction of M; remarks implying response source is intrinsic to blot or objects it resembles; vista (Phillips and Smith); exclusive form-determined R (Schafer-Rorschach); failure to turn cards; increment FC; M equals two times sum C, increment F (Klopfer-Davidson); R Cards VIII, IX, and X less than 30%. (Klopfer-Davidson; Klopfer-Developments I)

Inhibition of aggression:

Blot, spot content. (Phillips and Smith)

Inhibition in emotionally provocative situations possibly:

Decrement R, color cards. (Klopfer-Developments II)

Inhibition for fear of injury: Emblem content. (Klopfer-Developments I)

Inhibition of hostility: Making ferocious animals cartoon characters. (Schafer-Rorschach)

Inhibited normal subject: Delayed reaction time; low CF; low R in setting of good intelligence; M:C of 1:0; single response to Card X. (Schafer-Clinical Application)

Inhibition possibly: Form-determined response first. (Klopfer-Developments I)

Inhibition produced by anxiety: Hd content. (Beck III)

Intellectualization: Art content; Dd; Dd (edge details); remarks implying response source is intrinsic to blot or object it resembles; science content (Phillips and Smith); comments regarding percept of heads detached from body of person; exclusive form-determined R (Schafer-Rorschach); face and head Hd; side Dd profiles, Card I (Klopfer-Developments I); increment Dd. (Rapaport; Schafer-Rorschach)

Intellectualization defense possibly: Decrement R, increment W; increment F%; increment space; increment W; R 40+ (Schafer-Rorschach); remarks suggesting response is contingent and possible rather than certain. (Phillips and Smith)

Intellectualization of insight: Color description and color naming. (Klopfer-Davidson)

Intellectual pretentiousness: Excessive W. (Schafer-Clinical Application)

Intellectual resources which may be dissimulated or utilized for neurotic defense purposes only: FC only, equal number of M and FC, above average intelligence. (Schafer-Rorschach)

Isolation: Color denial (Beck III); bland detachment relative to both neutral and "taboo" or emotionally provocative responses; exclusive form-determined R; increment Dd. (Schafer-Rorschach)

Isolation defense possibly:	Comments regarding percept of head as detached from body of person; decrement color, shading, texture; detached but introspective test approach; high F+ and extended F+; increment F%; increment M+; machines, precision maneuvers, statue. (Schafer-Rorschach)
Lack of capacity for insight:	Decrement M. (Schafer-Rorschach)
Lack of introspection:	A greater than 50%. (Phillips and Smith)
Obsessive doubting:	Excessive M. (Schafer-Clinical Application)
Obsessive tendency:	Increment M with depression. (Rapaport)
Obsessive tendency with isolation, reaction-formation, undoing:	Increment Dd. (Beck III)
Overcompensation:	Increment W; mediocre but not vague form or increment F-. (Klopfer-Developments I)
Overcompliance:	Increment P. (Anderson-Beck)
Overcontrol:	M greater than FM, FM less than 1/2 M. (Klopfer-Developments I)
Overcontrol possibly:	Marked increment F% and F+. (Schafer-Rorschach)
Passive-compliance, possibly as a defense mechanism:	Exclusive FC. (Schafer-Rorschach)
Passive-dependent role regression as defense against hostility:	Shift from wild carnivorous animals to passive noncarnivorous animals. (Schafer-Rorschach)
Passive-regressive dependency wishes:	Shangri-la content. (Schafer-Rorschach)
Passive-submissive defenses against hostility possibly:	Parrot content; puppet content. (Schafer-Rorschach)
Passive-submissive or defense against passive-submissive needs:	Charging bull; powerful wings. (Schafer-Rorschach)

Passive-submissive defense system with authoritative persons:	Turning head rather than card to alter view of blot. (Schafer-Rorschach)
Passive-submissive needs which may be denied:	Heroic authority symbols. (Schafer-Rorschach)
Passivity, perhaps as a defense against hostility:	Jellyfish content; moth content; rabbit content; sheep content. (Phillips and Smith)
Pedantry:	Increment Dd (Klopfer-Developments I; Schafer-Rorschach); increment good-form Dd (Klopfer-Davidson); science content. (Phillips and Smith)
Perfectionistic tendency:	Dx; increment form-determined complex determinants (FC, FT, FY); decrement low-form complex determinants (C, CF, TF, YF, etc.); increment F+ (Schafer-Rorschach); good form, W above expectancy. (Phillips and Smith)
Persistence of defenses:	M greater than color. (Beck III)
Phobic tendency:	Excessive qualification. (Phillips and Smith)
Phobic tendency possibly:	Increment of A, and/or At content. (Beck III)
Possible weakness of repressive defenses:	Anxiety or disgust evoked by insect percepts. (Schafer-Rorschach)
Projection as a defense against superego conflict:	Ears and eyes content; pointing finger. (Schafer-Rorschach)
Projection of hostility tendency:	Spider content (Schafer-Rorschach); witch content. (Beck and Molish)
Projection (paranoid type):	Emphasizing that one side or area is different in content from the other corresponding (almost identical) area or side. (Schafer-Rorschach)
Projection, possible paranoid tendency, especially with figure-ground reversals:	Increment space. (Schafer-Rorschach)
Projection of subject's own feelings of inadequacy or weakness:	H with attributes suggesting weakness. (Schafer-Rorschach)

Rationalization:

Color naming. (Klopfer-Developments I)

Reaction-formation:

Increment Dd. (Schafer-Rorschach)

Reaction-formation possibly:

Increment R (Beck III); nonblatant religious H content. (Phillips and Smith)

Reaction-formation against hostility:

Blood content followed by baby or domestic animal or religious content; increment form-determined complex determinants (FC, FT, FY); decrement low-form complex determinants (C, CF, TF, YF, etc.); increment form-determined and FC responses; increment F+%; pixie heads in red area; sunrise in red. (Schafer-Rorschach)

Reaction-formation against hostility possibly:

Absence of any asperity or assertion; overcompliance with test procedure; increment R; Wx responses (Schafer-Rorschach); non-P bony anatomy content. (Phillips and Smith)

Reaction-formation tendency, possibly with undoing:

Shading shock. (Beck and Molish)

Regression (regressive tendency):

Alice in Wonderland content; bunny content; candy content; children content; children-bundled-up content; children's garment content; circus content; cradle content; dragon content; elves content; emaciated animal detail; fireworks content; good fairy content; ice cream content; increment children's storybook characters and figures; infant carnivorous animals; leggings content; ogre content; partially consumed animals and objects; Snow White content; wizard content (Schafer-Rorschach); bacteria content; bee content; germ content (Phillips and Smith); FM; M in Hd or Dd; M– (Beck III); increment FM (Klopfer-Developments I); M in A (Klopfer's

FM); M in form-minus animal movement (FM-); M in Hd. (Beck and Molish)

Regression of speech function possibly:

Very slow time for first response. (Beck III)

Rejection of the wish contained in the percept:

Inability to recall a percept. (Beck III)

Repression (repressive tendency):

Asking for reassurance; attitude that tests are "crazy"; average or decrement R; card rejections; decrement Dd, M, R, W; delayed reaction time; egocentric, naive responses; fabulization; inability to perceive D1 of Card III as human because of gap between lower and upper half; increment A and P; increment color, texture, and YF shading; long reaction time followed by reference on chromatic cards to meaninglessness of color; long reaction time and rejection; low F%; personal references; rejections; shift from H to A content; short total time for card (Schafer-Rorschach); CF-W responses, color description, color symbolism; decrement M or FM, form +; F greater than 50%; FM; M greater than two times sum C, F% greater than 50 (Klopfer-Developments I); color shock (Phillips and Smith, citing Rorschach); decrement M (Rapaport); decrement M and FM, increment F% (Beck and Molish); Hdx, slow response time (Beck and Molish); response increment to cool colors. (Beck III)

Repression (repressive tendency) possibly:

Appearance of response only during inquiry; long pause before response; impulsive, unreflective. (Schafer-Rorschach)

Repression of hostility:

Shift from wild carnivorous animals to passive noncarnivorous animals. (Schafer-Rorschach)

Repression of id impulses:

No FM. (Klopfer-Davidson)

Resistance to self-revelation; withholding of perceived material:

Reluctance to produce a response; demuring remarks but not refusal or stated inability. (Phillips and Smith)

Resistiveness as defense against inferiority feelings:

Space increment with vista. (Beck III)

Rigidity (inflexibility):

Approach narrow, rigid sequence; automatic phrases, no organic involvement; increment F+; increment qualification; lack of variability in time for first response; no turning; 100% F+; precision alternatives; stereotyped phrases; symmetry (Beck III); bony anatomy (Rapaport); decrement color, M, shading; high F% (50–80); narrow content range (Klopfer-Davidson); increment F+; increment P (Schafer-Rorschach); response time 40″ or more (Phillips and Smith); schizophrenic space. (Beck and Molish)

Rigidity possibly:

Anatomy and animal content; increment of animal content (Beck and Molish); complaint that all cards look alike (Schafer-Rorschach); low color and M in experience balance (coarctated EB); [Beck III]

Rigidity, with conscious and incessant efforts at self-control:

Ambiequal experience balance, no more than one color and M. (Beck and Molish)

Secretive:

Smiling at Rorschach cards but not examiner. (Phillips and Smith)

Severe inhibition:

Blocking, low productivity, rejections, slow response time, stereotypy (high A and AT%). (Beck and Molish)

Successful defense against hostility by compliance and meticulousness:

Increment Dd and FC+. (Schafer-Rorschach)

Suppression of hostility possibly:

Nonaggressive animals (dog, sheep, turtle). (Klopfer-Developments I)

Suspicion: Ears and eyes content (Beck and Molish); eyes content (Beck III; Phillips and Smith); looking at back of cards; more than two faces; mouth content. (Phillips and Smith)

Undoing: Blood content followed by overdeferential attitude toward the examiner; following response with anxious or hostile implications by one with more innocuous content (as "blood" followed by "jam"); qualifying response to make it more innocuous in significance, as "a devil; a friendly sort of devil" (Schafer-Rorschach); opposite qualities ascribed to a percept as "strong" or "weak" (Beck and Molish); precision alternatives with first rejected for second (Phillips and Smith); symmetry comments and responses. (Beck III)

Undoing possibly: Excessive or too-rapid verbalization followed by apologies or repeated questions as to whether verbalization is excessive or too rapid. (Schafer-Rorschach)

View of others as inferior in   Deformed heads content. (Schafer-Rorschach)
intelligence to subject possibly:

Withdrawal (withdrawal tendency):   Decrement color; low P with low sum color (Schafer-Clinical Application); popular humans of III perceived as animals (Schafer-Rorschach); absence of color responses in Cards VIII-X (Beck and Molish); color avoidance and denial; rejections; Y (Beck III); color responses less than non-color responses; M equals two times sum C, increment F; M greater than two times sum C, F% greater than 50 (Klopfer-Developments I); Dd M (Phillips and Smith); FY emphasis. (Klopfer-Davidson)

Withdrawal in presence of stimuli like that suggested by the card rejected:

Rejection without evidence of guardedness. (Schafer-Rorschach)

With increment and in Dd areas represent obsessive-compulsive denial, reaction-formation, undoing:

Hd facial expressions. (Beck and Molish)

Youth associations:

Flower bed. (Schafer-Rorschach)

Diagnostic Syndromes

ADDICTION
Addiction tendency:

Increment Dd (Rapaport); oral content. (Beck and Molish)

Alcohol addiction tendency ("alcoholics"):

Crab content; fish content; flower content; frog content; jellyfish content; lake, river, and stream content; lobster content; map content; octopus content; turtle content; seahorse content; snail content; water content; (Phillips and Smith); arbitrary color; eating, food and mouth content; F+ level low (Schafer-Clinical Application); increment water responses. (Beck and Molish)

Alcohol addiction, with symptoms of gastrointestinal complaints and history of early drinking:

Demanding and dependent behavior, irresponsibility, lack of attainment and perseverance. (Schafer-Clinical Application)

Neurotic alcoholics:

Hills content. (Phillips and Smith)

CHARACTER DISORDER
Antisocial acting out (especially with no M or shading):

Only color C. (Phillips and Smith)

Antisocial behavior possibly with increment:

Space in extratensive setting. (Beck and Molish)

Antisocial personality ("narcissistic character disorder" type):

Average or low R; avoidance of intellectual effort; bland self-references;

borderline F+ (60%); CF; decrement M; denial of obvious shading; evasion; food content; leering sexual references; low W% or vague W; ornamental content; sensuous T; egocentric, facetious, weak empathetic and introspective capacity; increment C with CF and FC.   (Schafer-Clinical Application)

Antisocial personality ("psychopaths, psychopathy, psychopathic character disorder"):

Absence of abstraction content; arbitrary and inappropriate FY; bee content; bird content; bug content; cockroach content; crab content; frog content; increment map content; ink, paint content; lobster content; M equals three times sum C; monkey content; multiple rejections (with guardedness); rough texture; sadistic content; stain content; tossing of card back to examiner; underproduction of M; visceral anatomy; weapon content (Phillips and Smith); apparent openness or sincerity with narcissistic use of color; great show of industry with banal responses and evasion (Schafer-Rorschach); CF exclusively; DW; D dominance; high animal percentage; history of law violations or disregard for ethical conduct, with blandness; lack of long-range goals and capacity for long-range goals; low F+%; perseveration and stereotypy of content; R 10–20; shading absent; simple schizophrenic pattern with high R, no peculiar verbalizations (Schafer-Clinical Application); decrement M and FM; mediocre or poor form (Klopfer-Developments I); increment P; W less than two times M. (Rapaport)

Antisocial personality ("psychopathy") with acting out, assaultiveness, lack of long-range goals:

Bug (beetle) content.   (Phillips and Smith)

Antisocial personality ("psychopathy") with guardedness:

Rejection of all ten cards, or all but one or two cards. (Phillips and Smith)

Antisocial personality ("psychopathy") with hostility:

Tossing back card. (Phillips and Smith)

Antisocial personality ("psychopathy") with overt sadistic acting out:

Aggressive implement content (machine guns, etc.) with other sadistic content. (Phillips and Smith)

Antisocial personality ("psychopathy") with sadism:

War content.   (Phillips and Smith)

Antisocial personality ("psychopathy") with sadism toward women:

Monkey content. (Phillips and Smith)

Antisocial or scheming tendency:

Fox content; rodent content. (Klopfer-Developments I)

Asthenic personality ("neurasthenia, neurasthenic"):

Decrement color; decrement F+; increment FV; increment rejections; narrow experience balance (Rapaport); low F% in constricted record (Schafer-Clinical Application); repulsion expressed to blot appearance. (Phillips and Smith)

Character disorder:

Increment Dd. (Rapaport)

Explosive personality ("emotional instability, explosiveness"):

Anxiety or disgust reaction with arbitrary or diffuse form (Schafer-Rorschach); at least 2–3 M present, minimal or no sum C; T, TF (Phillips and Smith); C and CF with low affective ratio; CF–, FC– (Beck III); CF (Rapaport); C greater than CF (Klopfer-Developments I); pure C (more than one) [Klopfer-Davidson; Klopfer-Developments I]; volcano. (Beck and Molish)

Hysterical personality ("hysterics, hysteria"):

C and CF with low affective ratio (Beck III); color first on III; color greater than M; increment F+; decrement M; increment CF; increment P (Rapaport); CF limited to blood, botany, clouds, and nature content; traits of histrionic behavior, lability, and naiveté (Schafer-Clinical Application); fabulization, frightening appearance (Phillips and Smith); inability to perceive responses to some blot areas, no difficulty with perception on other areas. (Klopfer-Developments I)

Inadequate personality ("inadequacy"):

Automaton content; badly baked cookie content; badly tied bow tie; bleeding, crushed, mutilated anatomy, animals, and persons; body without backbone content; botched or poorly prepared materials, ornaments, and specimens; bowed, debased, powerless, slovenly, subjugated persons; brassiere content; breastplate content; burdened animals and people content; carnivorous animals and insects; charms content; chess pawn content; clipped French poodle; cutting or squeezing implement; damaged, deteriorated, diseased animals or persons; damaged, deteriorated, frayed objects; dangling legs content; dead, missing, or mutilated human or plant limbs; dragon content; drooping arms; drooping or limp limbs and organisms; emaciated face; emaciated or tattered figures (beggar, scarecrow); fire and hell content; fleeing, frightening, and sinister animals, figures, and places; guiding beams content (beacon, lighthouse); hands raised in supplication; hell associations; helpless, powerless animals or figures; hut content; kneeling position content; lighthouse content; loss-of-grip associations; marionette content; parrot content; peasant content; performing animals and pets; prison bars; ragged or torn clothes;

robot content; scars and wounds content; servant content; supporting objects; symbols of imprisonment; tattered figures content; tortured persons; trained monkey content; wasteland content; wings too heavy or large for body; yoke content (Schafer-Rorschach); decrement D (Rapaport); lake content; stated inability to produce a response; vague W (map, X-ray). (Phillips and Smith)

Obsessive-compulsive personality ("compulsive, obsessive, obsessive-compulsive"):

Ambiequal experience balance; ambiequal experience balance, S increment (Beck III); excessive precision, pedantry, use of esoteric terms, face content; symmetry comments and responses; systematic examination and rotation (Phillips and Smith); exclusion of areas from F+ Dd percepts; bomb content (Klopfer-Developments II); Hd other than faces and heads (Klopfer-Developments I); high F+ (Klopfer-Davidson); increment of animal content, increment Dd (Rapaport; Schafer-Rorschach); increment M; increment M, no color (Schafer-Clinical Application); increment R; M greater than color. (Rapaport)

Obsessive-compulsive personality, with defenses of intellectualization, isolation, and rationalization:

Doubting rumination, excessive emotional constraint, pedantry. (Schafer-Clinical Application)

Paranoia ("paranoid condition"):

Contaminated W's; increment M; little or no color; over concern with similarity of cards; space responses in meager record; series of failures especially on last 3–4 cards; symbolic Dd. (Schafer-Clinical Application)

Paranoid personality ("paranoid character"):

Circumstantial descriptions; high A, F, F+, P%; legalistic attitude; low or no color; low M; much Dd and S; over-

preoccupation with similarities between cards; traits of overcaution and
suspicion. (Schafer-Clinical
Application)

Passive-aggressive ("oral-aggressive")
personality:

Animals or persons arguing, deriding,
spitting, sticking tongues out, yelling;
Atlas content; biting animals; brassiere
content; breastplate content; burdened
animals and people content; camel
content; cannibal content; carcass content; carnivorous animals and insects
content; clawing animals content; claws
content; cloaked women content; coyote content; crab content (other than
popular D, D7, and D8 of Card X); crocodile content; Dracula content; eagle's
beak content; emaciated face content;
emaciated or tattered figures (beggar,
scarecrow) content; false teeth content; fangs content; feeding animals
content; fighting animals content;
flat- or small-bosomed woman content; larva, locusts, other plant-devouring insects content; lion content;
man-weighted-down-by-pack content;
mouthless or toothless face content;
mule content; ox content; pit content;
preying animals content; pursuing
animals content; scarecrow content;
shark content; skull-of-steer-in-desert
content; snake (and other named
snake species); spider content; spider-
web content; tapeworm content; teeth
content; tiger content; tomato worm
content; trap content; tusks content;
vampire content; vise content; vulture
content; wasteland content; wild boar
content; witch content; woman with
enveloping cloak content; yoke content (Schafer-Rorschach); mouth content (Phillips and Smith); side D,

Card V, as crocodile head. (Klopfer-Developments I)

Schizoid personality ("schizoid, schizoid character , schizoid state"):

Blandness; dependence on fantasy gratification; excessive fabulization; high W; inverted percepts (seeing figures upside down or without reversing card); lack of object relations; no color or emphasis on color except limited arbitrary FC; peculiar verbalizations; several M; sex symbolism; with depression, low R; with sexual and somatic complaints, low F+, more At and sex content (Schafer-Clinical Application); decrement R, W to D ratio 2:1 (Rapaport); marionettes, puppets, Card III. (Phillips and Smith)

Schizoid personality possibly ("schizoid tendency"):

Absence of popular as first response, Card I; (Hd) content (Phillips and Smith); increment M with depression (Rapaport); perceiving cards as inverted; sex responses to limited number of usual areas. (Schafer-Clinical Application)

NEUROSIS
Anxiety neurosis ("anxiety, anxiety reaction, anxiety state"):

Apprehension; decrement color (1-2 CF, FC possibly); impaired attention and concentration, increased Dd; increment At, FY, and TF; moderately low F+; R greater than 20; rejection VIII, IX, X, and shaded cards; vague W (Schafer-Clinical Application); H equal to Hd; underproduction of M (F+ high, color and R below expectancy). (Phillips and Smith)

Anxiety neurosis ("anxiety state") with decompensation:

Anxiety neurosis with circumstantiality, compulsivity, and description. (Schafer-Clinical Application)

Depressed or dysphoric mood:

Death content; decay and desolation; mourning and weeping. (Schafer-Rorschach)

Depression if intelligence is average or above average:

Smoke content. (Phillips and Smith)

Depression possibly, with defeatist tendency:

Slave content. (Schafer-Rorschach)

Depression severe:

Accumulation of failures in Rorschach; decay (including fungus). (Schafer-Clinical Application)

Depressive introjection of hostility:

Criticism of self for unproductiveness. (Schafer-Rorschach)

Depressive neurosis ("depression, depressive"):

Absence or marked decrement of space; ambiequal M:C; decrement R and Z; increment F+ and low-form shading; no more than one C and M; resignation formulas, as "That's all I can think of"; slow time for first response; vista responses possibly (Beck III); absence of pure C; A increment; damage, death, and decay content; decrement color and M; derogatory self-references; dysphorically toned abstractions and fabulizations; emphasis on FY; F+ approaching 100% (high F+); high A%; Hd greater than H; impotency and perplexity; underproduction of M (F+, R, and color below expectancy); rejection Cards IV, V, VI (Phillips and Smith); anger with self, feelings of worthlessness, inertia; A greater than 50%; F% above 80; increased M with low productivity; long reaction time; low sum color (possibly one pure C, usually blood on II or III); low F% in constricted record; low W; no more than one M; P greater than 30%; R below 20, often below 15; rejections, self-criticism, or subtle criticisms of the test or examiner (Schafer-Clinical Application); clouds content; desolate landscapes (swamps, etc.), desolation; thunderstorm content (Schafer-Rorschach); cold objects and scenes (ice, snow, etc.); low color; shading increment (Beck and Molish); consistent self-depreciation; decrement color; decrement Dd; decrement M; decrement R; increment animal content; increment F+ D; increment F%; increment F+%; increment P; increment rejection; narrow experience balance; one M on III, none elsewhere (Rapaport); F% greater than 80, good form; FY emphasis; response time more than one minute (Klopfer-Davidson); Y. (Beck and Molish; Schafer-Rorschach)

Depressive neurosis ("depression") possibly:

Calling colors black; criticism of card with overpoliteness to examiner (Schafer-Rorschach); oral content (Beck and Molish); shock on Card IV; skeleton content (Klopfer-Developments I); skull content (Klopfer-Developments I; Schafer-Rorschach); stereotypy. (Rapaport)

Hypochondriacal neurosis (hypochondriachal complaints, hypochondriosis, pathologic concern with health):

Increment anatomy content (Beck III; Phillips and Smith); original anatomy content (Beck III); W anatomy, Card I.
(Klopfer-Developments I)

Hypochondriacal neurosis, severe ("severe hypochondriasis"):

Anatomy content with increment color; C and CF with low affective ratio (Beck III); blocking and delayed reaction on color or shaded cards; blood content on II and III; CF greater than FC; CF first on color cards and appears on II and III; CF limited to blood, botany, clouds, nature content; fabulization; frightening animals as King Kong, snakes, spiders; increment C with CF and FC;

low Dd and DW; R below 30; sum color above M and M is one or zero; traits of histrionic behavior, lability, naiveté ; Y and YF content (Schafer-Clinical Application); blood responses to achromatic areas; C and CF responses to red areas, often with expressed conflict over its use; fabulization; frightening appearance fabulization; low-form red, expressed dislike or hesitancy in its use; underproduction of M (Phillips and Smith); color first on III; color greater than M; decrement F+;decrement M;increment color; increment CF; increment F+%; increment P (Rapaport); inability to perceive responses to some blot areas, no difficulty with perception on other areas (Klopfer-Developments II); red shock followed by red-determined content (Boehm). [Beck and Molish]

Hysterical neurosis, conversion type ("conversion reaction, hysteria with conversion tendency"):

Underproduction of M (Phillips and Smith); extratensive experience balance in hysteric with anatomy content; increment anatomy content.
(Beck III)

Hysterical neurosis ("hysteric") and may indicate conversion tendency:

Blood content in achromatic areas.
(Phillips and Smith)

Hysterical neurosis ("hysteria") variations once basic hysterical syndrome is established:

With anatomical content, conversion; with high F+, compulsive tendencies; with increment M or M other than III, phobic tendencies; with low F+, anxiety and lability; with usual sex content, sexual preoccupation.
(Schafer-Clinical Application)

Hysterical neurosis possibly ("hysterical tendency, possible hysteria"):

Asking for reassurance; average or decrement R; blood content on II and III; decrement Dd, R, W; emotional reaction to response as reason why it was given; fabulization;

increment color, texture, and YF shading; long reaction time and rejection; low F%; personal references. (Schafer-Rorschach)

Hysteroid trend with obsessive defenses; or obsessive phobic anxiety:

Shading shock. (Beck and Molish)

Neurasthenic neurosis ("neurasthenia"):

Blocked or inactive M; diminutive animal content; disgust reaction to card; flexor M (Phillips and Smith); decrement color; decrement F+; increment FV; increment rejections; narrow experience balance (Rapaport); low F% in constricted record. (Schafer-Clinical Application)

Neurosis:

CF color; +1C; decrement H; decrement pleasantly toned shading; fabulization; Hd; negative response to color; shock on Card III; travel content (Phillips and Smith); color shock. (Beck and Molish; Beck III; Phillips and Smith, citing Rorschach)

Neurosis possibly:

Lack of variability in time for first response. (Beck III)

Neurosis severe, with felt neurotic distress:

Diseased anatomy content. (Schafer-Rorschach)

Obsessive ideas:

Increment M. (Schafer-Clinical Application)

Obsessive-compulsive neurosis ("compulsive, obsessive, obsessive-compulsive state"):

Ambiequal experience balance (color equal to M); precision alternatives; overemphasis on Dd (Beck and Molish); ambiequal experience balance, S increment; edging; increment Dd and R (Beck III); asking for further explanation of the Rorschach before performing; increment of A content; increment Dd; increment FC; increment M with neurosis; increment R; M greater than color (Rapaport); comments on asymmetry of cards; increment Dd; increment F+% (Schafer-Rorschach);

criticism of form adequacy of blot; decrement color with increment M; fabulization; F greater than 80%; F+ greater than 80%; increment Dd, Dx, M, S; increment M with low productivity; increment M, no color; no more than two rare M, one on III; over 50% A; R above 35; symmetry comment (Schafer-Clinical Application); decrement A + H, increment Ad + Hd; Hd other than faces and heads; increment Dd (Klopfer-Developments I); edge details; either-or alternatives; esoteric phrases and terms—pedantry; face content; H greater than Hd; inquiry by subject in regard to how he is expected to perform; lips content; precision alternatives; remarks implying response source is intrinsic to blot or objects it resembles; static M; symmetry comments and responses; systematic examination and rotation (Phillips and Smith); exclusion of areas from F + Dd percepts, banal content (Klopfer-Developments II); F% greater than 80, good form; high F+; increment good-form Dd.
(Klopfer-Davidson)

Obsessive-compulsive neurosis decompensating:

Increment C with CF and FC.
(Schafer-Clinical Application)

Obsessive-compulsive neurosis possibly:

Increment perplexed qualification; symmetry comments and responses.
(Schafer-Rorschach)

Obsessive-compulsive neurosis with defenses of intellectualization, isolation, and rationalization:

Doubting rumination, excessive emotional constraint, pedantry.
(Schafer-Clinical Application)

Obsessive-compulsive neurosis with doubting and rituals possibly:

Ambiequal experience balance (color equal to M). [Beck and Molish]

Obsessive-compulsive neurosis with Fm may suggest possible homosexual fears:

War content. (Phillips and Smith)

Obsessive-compulsive neurosis in hysteria ("compulsive tendencies in hysterics"):

Hysterical features with high F+. (Schafer-Clinical Application)

Obsessive-compulsive neurosis with obsessive rumination ("obsessive rumination"):

Shading shock. (Beck and Molish)

Phobic anxiety:

Color-shading blends, Card IX. (Beck and Molish)

Phobic neurosis ("phobia, phobic tendency"):

Anxiety or disgust evoked by insect percepts (Schafer-Rorschach); biting A content; mouth content; teeth content; black bat content (Beck III); color denial (Klopfer-Developments II); Hd greater than M (Phillips and Smith); hysterical features with increment M or M other than on III; monster content (Schafer-Clinical Application); M greater than color (Rapaport); snakes, wolves, and other threatening animals. (Beck and Molish)

Phobic neurosis ("phobic") if aggressive in content:

Hd facial expressions. (Beck and Molish)

Phobic neurosis ("phobic") possibly, if H is frightening:

Fairy tale entities. (Beck and Molish)

Phobic neurosis ("phobic, phobic tendency") possibly:

Emotional reaction to response as reason why it was given (Schafer-Rorschach); increment anatomy content; increment animal content; snake (and other named snake species); wolf content (Beck III); use of term "weird." (Schafer-Rorschach)

Somatization tendency:

Anatomy, Card VIII (Klopfer-Developments I); CF; FY; increment anatomy content (Rapaport); W anatomy, Card I. (Klopfer-Developments I)

Somatic complaints:

Edging, shock, Card III.
(Phillips and Smith)

ORGANICITY
Organic brain syndrome ("brain
damage, organicity, organics"):

Accumulation of failures in Rorschach
(Schafer-Clinical Application); Adx
and Hdx; absence of qualification;
combination of space with nonspace
areas in crude undifferentiated response; decrement of M; deterioration
content; distractability; doubt expressed about adequacy of a percept;
extreme confabulation; extreme DW
responses; inappropriate color ("green
fire"); incongruent, irrelevant conver-
sational remarks; rocks and stones
content; underproduction of M (Phillips and Smith); C and CF with low
affective ratio; stereotyped phrases
(Beck III); combination of predomi-
nant FC with crude CF and C; deterioration content; early appearance of
shading; facetiousness with self-distrust; rejection of Card III with H
elsewhere; rejection of part of human
figure on Card VII; response perseveration; war and violence themes
(representing fear of loss of control.)
(Klopfer-Developments II)

Organic brain syndrome, best of the
Piotrowski signs for mild to moderate
brain damage:

Piotrowski's automatic phrases; impotence, perplexity, and repetition.
(Klopfer-Developments I)

Organic brain syndrome,
classical signs:

Automatic phrases; less than 15 R;
mostly W responses; not more than
one M; perplexity; projection emphasis; response time over one minute.
(Klopfer-Developments I)

Organic brain syndrome ("brain
damage"), early type possibly:

Evidence of anxiety despite security.
(Klopfer-Developments II)

Organic brain syndrome, frontal
lesion possibly:

Change of personality reported with
evidence of brain damage; crudeness,

poor judgment, absence of other evidence of brain damage; evidence of concreteness plus poor judgment. (Klopfer-Developments II)

Organic brain syndrome ("brain damage"), frontal lobe; or retardation:

Adx and Hdx. (Phillips and Smith)

Organic brain syndrome, generalized cortical damage or subcortical involvement:

Both visual and motor disturbance. (Klopfer-Developments II)

Organic brain syndrome, geriatric patients:

Constriction, stereotypy; decrement D, increment vague W; increment animal content (Klopfer-Developments I); decrement M, shading, texture; increment F; decrement R, increment time required for response; lack of color or emphasis on CF and C. (Klopfer-Developments II)

Organic brain syndrome, grand mal seizures possibly:

Passive content Rorschach, aggressive TAT content. (Klopfer-Developments I)

Organic brain syndrome, metastasized cerebral carcinoma or multiple sclerosis:

Good Wechsler, poor Rorschach performance. (Klopfer-Developments I)

Organic brain syndrome, more likely to occur with brain-damaged than with schizophrenic patients:

Selection of common areas for percept. (Klopfer-Developments I)

Organic brain syndrome, multiple sclerosis possibly:

Inconsistent evidence of hysteria. (Klopfer-Developments II)

Organic brain syndrome, parietal-temporal lesion possibly:

Visual disturbance with evidence of crudity, or motor disturbance, or poor judgment. (Klopfer-Developments II)

Organic brain syndrome, parietal temporal lesion possibly:

Adequate Block Design and Bender performance, disturbed speech. (Klopfer-Development II)

Organic brain syndrome ("brain damage, organicity") possibly:

Color naming (Rapaport); perseveration of organic content (Klopfer-

Developments II); rocks (Phillips and Smith); T.
(Klopfer-Developments I)

Organic brain syndrome, post-traumatic brain damage:

Inability to give alternate interpretations to some blot area.
(Klopfer-Developments II)

Organic brain syndrome, relatively valid signs of brain damage:

Anxious, self-derogatory comments; catastrophic reactions; confusion of background and foreground; covering parts of blot with hand to expose other areas more conspicuously; discrepancy poor performance on Rorschach as compared to Wechsler test; emphasis on projections; inability to give alternative responses to same area; inappropriate combination of good response to adjacent areas; coherence and reasonable associational sequence (to rule out schizophrenia) with inability to give alternate responses to the same area; passive content Rorschach with aggressive TAT content; perseverated CF content on last three cards; repeated personal references; silly responses accompanied by sensible remarks; use of shading in Card I and II; vague W with good-form Dd details; variability in response quality.
(Klopfer-Developments II)

Organic brain syndrome, relatively valid signs for mild-to-moderate brain damage:

Concern about body image as reflected in deterioration comments or fragmentation of H content.
(Klopfer-Developments I)

Organic brain syndrome, severe brain damage:

Anal and water content, projected regression, susceptibility to fatigue.
(Klopfer-Developments II)

Organic brain syndrome, severe brain damage possibly:

Decrease of anxiety with evidence of brain damage.
(Klopfer-Developments II)

Organic brain syndrome, small focal lesion, usually accompanied by seizure:

Emphasis on projections. (Klopfer-Developments II)

Organic brain syndrome, toxic states:

Absurd content presented in jovial manner, along with more sensible comments. (Klopfer-Developments II)

PSYCHOPHYSIOLOGIC DISORDERS

Psychophysiologic disorders:

Color below expectancy; increment F+; low-form color; decrement M; F+ color below expectancy; non-P bony anatomy content; reduction R, mediocre W increment; static M; sum C 3–4 times M; underproduction of M (high F+, R, and color) (Phillips and Smith); extratensive EB; increment F+: M approximately equal to FM, no color.
(Klopfer Developments I)

PSYCHOSIS

Acting-out psychosis probably with large labile, negativistic element and severely impaired emotional control:

Decrement A, F+, FC, H, M, P, increment C, CF-, S. (Beck and Molish)

Acute schizophrenia or chronic undifferentiated schizophrenic episode ("unclassified schizophrenia, panic states"):

Adequate F+ with occasional arbitrary form; arbitrary FC (early disappearance FC unfavorable prognostic sign); balanced color and M; breakdown of reality testing, confusion, disorganized thinking; CF; confabulation; contamination; peculiar verbalizations; R 20–30; shading with schizophrenic disorganization.
(Schafer-Clinical Application)

Bizarre impulsive behavior:

Pure C with low A% and F%.
(Schafer-Clinical Application)

Blocked or paranoid schizophrenia:

Accumulation of failures in Rorschach.
(Schafer-Clinical Application)

Cautious paranoid:

Increment M with low productivity.
(Schafer-Clinical Application)

Chronicity:

Dd M; M in Hd. (Phillips and Smith)

Contraindicates psychosis, except guarded early paranoid schizophrenia:

Shading denial.   (Klopfer-Developments II)

Delusional, if psychosis is present:

M greater than color. (Rapaport)

Delusional symptoms (delusional tendency):

Increment M, no color (Schafer-Clinical Application); increment M (many M's) with psychosis (schizophrenic disorganization) [Rapaport; Schafer-Clinical Application] ; smiling at Rorschach cards but not at examiner. (Phillips and Smith)

Depersonalization tendency:

Death, dehumanization, mutilation content. (Beck III)

Deteriorated schizophrenia:

Arbitrary and inappropriate FY; inappropriate color (green fire). [Phillips and Smith]

Disruption in formal thought processes:

Dd perseveration. (Phillips and Smith)

Eccentricity probably, rather than psychosis:

O-, good form.   (Klopfer-Developments I)

Effort to maintain reality contact in latent schizophrenia ("incipient schizophrenic") with break probable:

Emotionality displayed, without color on Rorschach.   (Schafer-Clinical Application)

Expansiveness, possible grandiosity:

Confabulation, decrement F+; increment W. (Schafer-Rorschach)

Grandiose aspirations possibly, unless F-:

Increment W.   (Schafer-Rorschach)

Grandiosity:

W:M ratio 3:1. (Phillips and Smith)

Grandiosity and paranoid attitudes possibly:

Increment arbitrary W.   (Schafer-Rorschach)

Grandiosity possibly:

Making things large that are usually seen as small (a "big mouse," etc.). (Schafer-Rorschach)

Intellectualizing paranoid:

Expansiveness, grandiosity, high R, high W. (Schafer-Clinical Application)

Manic tendency:

Affective ratio or percent color of about 80 or more. (Beck III)

Paranoid syndromes ("paranoid tendency"):

Abstract responses that require perceptual reorganization; symbolic content in sexual areas (Schafer-Clinical Application); Adx and Hdx; bee content; cloaking and disguising garments; eagle content; eyes content; excessive Dd M; face Hd to space area (paranoid schizophrenic); fly content; full-face Hd (paranoid schizophrenic); high increment M; looking suspiciously at card back; M greater than C, also antisocial personalities ("psychopaths"); mouth content; sex content in schizophrenic men; suspicious remarks about purpose of evaluation or nature of stimulus; visceral anatomy content (vague unsystematized paranoid attitudes); visceral anatomy content (especially on Cards I, VIII, IX, X) [Phillips and Smith]; armor content; attributing to test or to examiner's attitude or assumed expectation responses unacceptable to patient, although produced by him; blood stains; celebrated or powerful persons or religious figures content; coat of arms content; comments on hidden meanings and similarities in or between cards; concealed, engulfing, and obscured figures content; concealing darkness content; crouching or fleeing figures content; crowns, emblems, and other kingly paraphernalia content; destroyed objects content; detectives or police content; electrical waves or rays content; evasion; eyes content; eyes perceived as "looking at" the subject; fangs content; fingers or footprint content;

finger pointing content; increment Dd content; instruments of torture or tortured persons content; jaws content; mask content; meager record; monuments content; mutilated parts content; overelaboration tiny D; pit content; poison content; religious figures; shells of animal content; sinister faces content; suspicion; symmetry comments; teeth content; trap content; web content (Schafer-Rorschach); asking for further explanation of Rorschach before performing; increment F%; increment F+; increment rejections (Rapaport); cloaking garments content; elevated Z score and increment F– with S; eyes; facial expression of hostility on same-sex figure; listening, peering, or staring H or Hd; the devil (Beck III); ears and eyes content (Beck and Molish); unwillingness to admit percept until convinced others see it. (Klopfer-Developments II)

Paranoid tendency possibly:

Abstract and symbolic figures and letters; ambiguous sex differences; arrowhead content; buttocks content; extremely large penis; figures seen from rear; gigantic penis; increment A, Ad, At, Hd; increment confabulation; lipstick content; phallic symbols, as arrow, cannon, spear; reversal of sex of figure or of sexual anatomy usually seen; small M (Schafer-Rorschach); aggressive A; decrement F+; H with paranoid content themes; high Z score; internal anatomy content; increment S (Beck III); anal anatomy content (Klopfer-Developments I; Klopfer-Davidson); buttocks content (Klopfer-Developments I;

Klopfer-Davidson; Schafer-Rorschach); decrement FV; increment space (Rapaport); ghost content. (Phillips and Smith)

Paranoid tendency appearing involutionally:

Eagle content. (Phillips and Smith)

Paranoid tendency with constriction and guardedness:

Increment F%; increment F+; decrement color and especially of CF; Fm; M-. (Schafer-Rorschach)

Paranoid tendency, especially with DW:

M-.   (Schafer-Clinical Application)

Persistence of delusions in patients:

Figure ground reversal space. (Beck III)

Potential catatonic excitement possibly:

Shading increment with C and S. (Beck and Molish)

Psychosis:

Bizarre form content; color areas, Card II; color naming; mediocre or poor form (Klopfer-Developments I); Dd perseveration; low F+; M in Dd areas; M- increment; M-:M ratio 1:3; pure C responses possibly; suspicious remarks about content of card or intent of examiner (Phillips and Smith); decrement F+, increment M. (Rapaport)

Psychotic delusions:

Blatant religious Human or Inhuman-Human content (God, etc.). [Phillips and Smith]

Psychotic depressive reaction ("psychotic depression"):

Decrement F+ and animal; increment At and vague form responses; decrement R, W to D ratio 1:2; increment C with depression (Rapaport); high At, low F+ with some individuals, otherwise high F+%; perhaps some confabulation in persons with depressive pattern (Schafer-Clinical Application); zero color and M. (Phillips and Smith)

Reality testing impaired:

Decrement D and P, poor form; decrement D and W, Dd increment;

	form-minus color without subjective discomfort; inability to see Card V as bat or butterfly; O-, poor form (Klopfer-Developments I); decrement of populars; extended F+ below 80%; low-form vague W's; perceptual vagueness (Schafer-Rorschach); inability to see P on testing limits; O-. (Klopfer-Davidson)
Reality testing impaired in emotionally stimulating situations:	FC-. (Klopfer-Davidson)
Reality contact possibly impaired:	Absence of color responses in Cards VIII- X; CF-; M- (Beck and Molish); decrement color, increment M (Rapaport); DW tendency, poor form; rejection of P after verbalizing it. (Schafer-Rorschach)
Religious delusions:	Religion content. (Phillips and Smith)
Represents paranoia in schizophrenia:	M greater than average. (Phillips and Smith)
Schizophrenia:	Absurdities; C greater than CF + FC; confabulation and contamination; deviant verbalizations; extremely irregular sequence; F+ less than 60%, especially less than 50%; increment sex content or reference to sex act; marked variability in quality and quantity of response; mutilated C; plural form for single percept (bats for bat, etc.); sex response to Card I, first response (Schafer-Clinical Application); anal content; bacteria content; bee content; bizarre equivalents and bizarreness; comment on inquiry that blot no longer looks like original percept; contamination; decrement H content (except paranoid); Dd perseveration; detached mouth content; fly content; food content; full-face space and full-face content (paranoid);

generalized visceral anatomy content; germ content; inappropriate color, as "green fire"; inappropriate elaborations; increment M– (favorable prognosis); increment religion content; increment sex content; inner details; low F+ and poor-form responses; low-form color; morbid content; mouth alone content; mumbling; mutilated anatomy; mutilated leaf content; negative form responses; negative percepts ("It's not a __"); overproduction of M (paranoid); peculiar and pedantic prefatory remarks; pure C (more than one); rejection VIII, IX, X; color response to yellow blot areas (poor form); sex content; travel content; visceral anatomy content, especially on Cards I, VIII, IX, X (Phillips and Smith); color greater than M; confabulation; contamination; decrement D; increment pure C; increment pure C, IX and X; narrow experience balance; pure C on Card VIII (Rapaport); confabulation; contamination; increment sex content or references to sex; low F+; M–; pure C (Schafer-Rorschach); decayed anatomy and diseased anatomy (Phillips and Smith; Schafer-Clinical Application); decrement D, vague form; W followed by Dd (Klopfer-Developments I); devastating fires; low P; objects collapsing (Beck III); F– response to color; response perseveration (Klopfer-Developments II); increment poor-form W. (Klopfer-Davidson)

Schizophrenia, catatonic type: Extreme confabulation (Phillips and Smith); perseverated F– color with detached affect; transposition (perceiving usual F+ content of an area in an area where the form becomes F-). (Klopfer-Developments II)

Schizophrenia, catatonic type, with potential for excitement if color is present:

Color, S, shading in schizophrenic record. (Beck and Molish)

Schizophrenia, chronic undifferentiated type ("chronic schizophrenia; unclassified schizophrenia"):

C greater than CF; CF greater than FC (Rapaport); decrement M, P; deterioration color responses; deviant reasoning; F+ below 60%; increment At, C, peculiar verbalizations, sex, shading (with schizophrenic tendency increment of shading yields potential for bizarre panic attacks); neologisms; no M; Po responses; pure C (Schafer-Clinical Application); primitive bizarre content without anxiety. (Schafer-Rorschach)

Schizophrenia, especially hebephrenic:

Dehumanized content; deterioration color. (Rapaport)

Schizophrenia (except paranoid):

Decrement F+; increment FV. (Rapaport)

Schizophrenia with excitement potential:

C and CF with low affective ratio. (Beck III)

Schizophrenia, or loose contact with reality:

Recognition of Rorschach percept as untenable, followed by its reaffirmation. (Schafer-Clinical Application)

Schizophrenia possibly:

Alphabet content; DW tendency; increment travel content (Phillips and Smith); breast content; lack of variability in time for first response (Beck III); increment anatomy content; increment DW or vague W. (Rapaport)

Schizophrenia, hebephrenic type:

Extreme confabulation. (Phillips and Smith)

Schizophrenia, latent type ("incipient schizophrenia"):

Abrupt change of an H to (H); apprehension with evidence of fantasy withdrawal; bizarre and dramatic abstractions of physical sensations;

confabulations, a couple of, with aggressive or sexual content; confusion; decay content; depersonalization; emotionality displayed without color on the Rorschach; geometric shape or letter content; grossly disparate M : C ratios; many anal and sex responses; many M's without high intelligence; no more than two arbitrary FC (as green sheep); no more than two M-; panic attacks (with delusions, psychotic break may be imminent); peculiar verbalizations, a few, which may be recognized as such; pure C's, a few; recognition of Rorschach percept as untenable, followed by its reaffirmation.   (Schafer-Clinical Application)

Schizophrenia, latent type ("latent schizophrenia"), or chronic undifferentiated schizophrenia possibly ("pseudo-neurotic schizophrenia"):

Color shock in schizophrenic record. (Beck and Molish)

Schizophrenia moving into remission:

Color naming. (Klopfer-Developments I)

Schizophrenia, paranoid type:

Absence florid schizophrenic verbalizations; alphabet letters; confabulation; constrictive tendency; contamination; decrement color, emphasis on M; Dd increment; eyes; F+ adequate unless blocking or perseverations occur; high A, F%; P; ideas of reference relative to intent of blot configuration; latent schizophrenic symptoms with caution and constriction; limited peculiar verbalizations; M-; M 2-3; no color; possible FC; symbols such as alphabet letters or geometric shapes; R below 25 or often below 15 (Schafer-Clinical Application); edge details; full-face Hd in space (except IX, Dds 29, seen by eccentric normals) [Phillips and Smith] ;

increment space in schizophrenic pattern (Beck and Molish); transposition (perceiving usual F+ content of an area in an adjacent area where the form becomes F-). [Klopfer-Developments II]

Schizophrenia, paranoid type (may be assaultive):

M equals three times sum C. (Phillips and Smith)

Schizophrenia, simple type ("simple schizophrenia"):

Absurd form responses; decrement M; DW; F+ 60%; failures or perseverations; high A or At; lack of rapport and emotional responsiveness, loss of interest, thinking peculiarities; low F+, P, R, with blandness; peculiar verbalizations; perseverations (one or more M or Dd's suggest vague delusions) [Schafer-Clinical Application]; decrement color, Dd, R; increment F%, P, rejections. (Rapaport)

Schizophrenic ambivalence:

Abstract, irrelevant dichotomy responses, as "life–death." (Beck and Molish)

Schizophrenic bizarreness:

Contaminations, extreme vagueness, grandiosity, non sequiturs. (Phillips and Smith, citing Rapaport)

Schizophrenic morbidity possibly:

Decay (including fungus). [Schafer-Clinical Interpretation]

Severe pathology, including schizophrenia:

Alphabet content. (Phillips and Smith)

Sporadic breakdown and reinstitution of controls, as with ambulatory schizophrenics and manics:

M balancing sum C. (Schafer-Clinical Application)

Systematized delusional potential as M diminshed with chronicity:

Decrement M, chronic undifferentiated schizophrenia ("unclassified schizophrenia"). [Schafer-Clinical Application]

Thought and judgment disturbance, possible psychosis:

Dd as first response to two or more cards. (Phillips and Smith)

Expressive Behavior

Assertiveness but with fear of rejection from others:	Peninsula content. (Phillips and Smith)
Blocked self-expression with inhibition of hostility:	Static M. (Phillips and Smith)
Creative potential not adequately expressed:	W less than two times M. (Klopfer-Davidson)
Excessive control of spontaneity; lack of uninhibited responsiveness:	FC greater than CF. (Klopfer-Davidson)
Expressivity:	M greater than S. (Phillips and Smith)
Freedom of self-expression:	Card turning without inquiry as to whether it's permissible, after developing previous response. (Phillips and Smith)
Inhibition of potential capacity:	Additional M, with decrement M. (Klopfer-Davidson)
Inhibition of self-expression with lack of determination and drive:	Cut-off W. (Phillips and Smith)
Lack of assertion:	Jellyfish content; rabbit content (Phillips and Smith); increment FC, no other color. (Rapaport)
Lack of spontaneity:	Dd (Phillips and Smith); detached but introspective test approach; exclusive FC; stylized figures, Card III, D1 (Schafer-Rorschach); FC only or almost exclusively; F% greater than 80, good form (Klopfer-Davidson); increment FC, minimum or no C or CF; M greater than FM, FM less than 1/2M (Klopfer-Developments I); increment FC, no other color (Rapaport); increment F% (Rapaport; Schafer-Rorschach); increment F+. (Beck III)
Overcompliance:	Increment FC, no other color. (Rapaport)
Overcontrol of impulses possibly:	Increment form-determined and FC responses. (Schafer-Rorschach)

Some freedom of self-expression:

Turning cards without asking permission. (Phillips and Smith)

Spontaneity:

M approximately equal to FM, CF present.   (Klopfer-Developments I)

Sponaneity possibly:

CF.   (Klopfer-Davidson; Klopfer-Developments I)

Tensions blocking constructive self-expression:

Additional FM, decrement FM. (Klopfer-Davidson)

Intellectual Status

Above average or superior intelligence:

Bay and harbor content; fabulization content; face content; iron ore content; M in abstraction; nature content; nonchildren's-literature H; peninsula content; scarab content; science content; scorpion; W equal to M (Phillips and Smith); diverse range of F+; whimsical content (Beck and Molish); wide content range. (Klopfer-Davidson)

Average intelligence or above:

Elaboration of basic percept; precision alternatives; preliminary remarks connoting hesitation; remarks suggesting response is contingent and possible rather than certain; symmetry comments and responses; totem pole content. (Phillips and Smith)

Cultural interests with above average intelligence:

Mythology content.   (Phillips and Smith)

Retardation ("low intelligence, mental defectives, retardates"):

Absence or decrement F+ originals; arbitrary and inappropriate FY; confabulation; decrement of M; food content; inferior form elaboration; inferior organization; low F+; "smoke" content; underproduction of M (Phillips and Smith); A greater than 50%; increment poor-form W; narrow content range; response time more than one minute (Klopfer-Davidson);

automatic phrases; H greater than Hd (Beck and Molish); color naming (Klopfer-Developments I); increment A content; increment P. (Rapaport)

Superior intelligence with more than one:

Music content. (Phillips and Smith)

Norms

Adolescents:

Travel content. (Phillips and Smith)

Adults 4%; catatonics and hebephrenics 3%; paranoids 15%:

Dd%. (Phillips and Smith, citing Friedman, H. and S.)

Adults 25%, catatonics and hebephrenics 46%; paranoids 16%:

W%. (Phillips and Smith, citing Friedman, H. and S.)

Adults 67% or catatonics and hebephrenics 45%; paranoids 67%:

Dd%. (Phillips and Smith, citing Friedman, H. and S.)

Age 7–8:

Emergence of fantasy activity. (Beck and Molish)

Analysands:

Anal content. (Phillips and Smith)

Anxious adolescents:

Devasting fires, objects collapsing. (Beck III)

At least three:

Optimal M. (Klopfer-Davidson)

Average 2 : 1:

W:M. (May drop as W+ or M increases.) (Phillips and Smith)

Begins at three years of age:

Use of color. (Klopfer-Developments II)

Characteristic of two-to three-year-old:

Perseveration of concepts, rejections. (Klopfer-Developments I)

Characteristic of four-to five-year-old child:

No perseveration of concepts except color responses to last three cards. (Klopfer-Developments II)

Children:

Bcc content; children's-literature content; completely unmodified, unqualified, terse responses; fly content; recreation content (Phillips and Smith); color naming, decrement M and FM; FC–; mediocre or poor form. (Klopfer-Developments I)

Common in children 4–7 years of age:

Confabulation. (Klopfer-Developments I)

Dd expectancy (average R):

5–15%. (Phillips and Smith)

DdM + M in A+ MHd + M– equal to less than one:

Optimal M to other determinants (M at expectancy). [Phillips and Smith]

Equal.

Ratio optimal H to M. (Phillips and Smith)

Erratic thinking:

O+75%. (Klopfer-Davidson)

15–35%:

W expectancy (average R). [Phillips and Smith]

FC to M ratio about equal, with FC:CF + C ratio 2:1:

Optimal M to other determinants (M at expectancy). [Phillips and Smith]

40–80%:

Normal range for affective ratio. (Beck III)

Four to six:

P frequency. (Phillips and Smith)

Four (more with superior intelligence); lower number H among schizophrenics, except paranoids; also below expectancy in psychotic depression and with anxiety and neurosis, except obsessive-compulsive:

Optimal H. (Phillips and Smith)

55–65%:

D expectancy (average R). [Phillips and Smith]

Five to seven years of age:

Increase of D. (Klopfer-Developments I)

FC ratio to CF + C is 2:1; spontaneity with mature impulse control:

Optimal color. (Phillips and Smith)

Insecurity in children:

Fire content. (Beck III)

Minimum for neurotic range:

F% of 60. (Beck III)

Less than H, less than three:

Optimal Hd. (Phillips and Smith)

More common in adolescents and children:

Gums and teeth content. (Klopfer-Davidson)

Neurotic range of reality contact:

F+ 60–70%. (Beck and Molish)

One (skeletal form):

Optimal range 1-3:

Optimal 25-40%, but decreases as intelligence and M increases:

Optimal 70% plus:

Optimum 2:1:

Phobic tendency in children:

Rare content:

Self-consciously nonconformist subject:

Significantly high increment of S:

Sum C:M about equal:

20-50%, objectivity:

35%, or 20-50%:

20-35%:

20-30%:

Two times popular (with at least five P):

Two to one:

Two to four years of age:

Two (more is inhibiting and associated with excessive self-criticality):

Up to age five:

Up to six years of age:

W: 20-30%; D: 45-55%; Dd: 0-15%:

Expected At%.   (Phillips and Smith)

Landscape content.   (Phillips and Smith)

A%. (Phillips and Smith)

F+. (Phillips and Smith)

(A + H)   :   (Ad + Hd).   (Klopfer-Davidson)

Fire content. (Beck III)

Implement content; mineral content. (Phillips and Smith)

Anal content.   (Phillips and Smith)

S–plus 10%. (Beck III)

Optimal M to other determinants (M at expectancy).   [Phillips and Smith]

F% optimum range. (Klopfer-Davidson)

Optimal F.   (Klopfer-Davidson; Klopfer-Developments I)

Optimal A. (Klopfer-Davidson)

Average R.   (Phillips and Smith)

Optimal O+. (Klopfer-Davidson)

Optimum FM:M. (Phillips and Smith)

Decrease of W; vague W. (Klopfer-Developments II)

Optimal vista.   (Phillips and Smith)

Color naming. (Klopfer-Developments II)

Global perception. (Klopfer-Developments II)

Form-plus optimum or expected range. (Klopfer-Developments I)

W:M ratio 2:1:	Ambition for accomplishment with potential for it. (Klopfer-Davidson)
W+ to M 1:1; W:M ratio 2:1:	Optimal M to other determinants (M at expectancy). [Phillips and Smith]
Women subjects:	Household content. (Phillips and Smith)
Young children:	Inappropriate color (green fire) [Phillips and Smith] ; M in Hd (Beck and Molish); W followed by Dd. (Klopfer-Developments I)

Object Relations

Ambivalence:	Ambiequal experience balance (color equal to M); opposite qualities ascribed to a percept, as "strong" and "weak"; symmetry comments and responses (Beck and Molish); ambiequal experience balance, S increment (Klopfer-Developments I); complimentary remarks about cards followed by disparaging comments; failure to turn card after asking permission. (Phillips and Smith)
Ambivalence with associated anxiety:	Static M. (Beck III)
Ambivalence with conflict possibly:	Comments on asymmetry of cards. (Schafer-Rorschach)
Ambivalence toward domineering father:	Ape content; bison (or buffalo); bull content; horse content; monkey content; tiger content. (Phillips and Smith)
Ambivalence toward domineering father, with concomitant suspicious attitudes, especially toward men:	Eagle content. (Phillips and Smith)
Ambivalence toward domineering father, with derogatory content:	Gorilla content. (Schafer-Rorschach)

Ambivalence toward male figure possibly:	Dead branch content. (Schafer-Rorschach)
Ambivalence toward maternal figure:	Edging, shock, Card I. (Phillips and Smith)
Ambivalence possibly toward aging, death, or impotence of male figure:	Dead branch content. (Schafer-Rorschach)
Antagonism toward (and fear of) maternal figure:	Spider content. (Klopfer-Davidson)
Anxiety relative to attitude toward same-sex parent:	Shock on Cards I and IV. (Beck and Molish)
Anxiety over frustrated need for affection:	V + VF. (Klopfer-Davidson)
Apprehension and feelings of inadequacy relative to paternal figure, especially if response is long for subject:	"Big feet" usual D on IV. (Schafer-Rorschach)
Appropriate emotional responsivity:	FC. (Klopfer-Davidson)
Appropriate response in social interaction:	FC > C + CF (Klopfer-Developments I); optimum P. (Beck and Molish)
Avoidance of social interaction:	(H) + 1 (Phillips and Smith); avoidance of H content. (Klopfer-Davidson)
Capacity for empathy, rapport:	FC (Rapaport; Beck and Molish); optimal M production. (Phillips and Smith)
Cautious interpersonal relations:	Mask content; mouse content; rabbit content; turtle content. (Schafer-Rorschach)
Conception of mother as destructive:	Spider content. (Schafer-Rorschach)
Concern over social role:	Clothing content. (Phillips and Smith)
Constrained emotional tone:	Walls content. (Schafer-Rorschach)
Constrained but reasonably comfortable social interaction:	F% about 50, F + FT + FV 75% or below. (Klopfer-Davidson)
Demanding, domineering, overprotective but not punitive maternal figure:	Edging, shock, Card VIII. (Phillips and Smith)
Deprivation of affection:	Chicken content. (Schafer-Rorschach)

Derision of women possibly:

Cow content. (Beck III)

Derogatory attitude toward femininity: a view of women as passive-oral in nature:

D1, Card V, pig's feet. (Schafer-Rorschach)

Derogatory attitudes toward others:

Human popular D3 as clowns or witches. (Klopfer-Developments I)

— Detached emotional tone:

Polar bear content. (Schafer-Rorschach)

Detachment:

Absence of elaboration, avoidance of additional responses to cards, terse style; remarks implying response is intrinsic to blot or objects it resembles; smiling at Rorschach cards but not at examiner (Phillips and Smith); Eskimo content (Schafer-Rorschach); R cards VIII, IX, and X < 30%. (Klopfer-Davidson; Klopfer-Developments I)

Detachment, coldness:

Arctic and winter associations. (Schafer-Rorschach)

Detachment, formal attitude toward others:

Stylized figures, Card VII, D1. (Schafer-Rorschach)

Difficulty with close relations with others:

Popular humans of Card III perceived as animals. (Schafer-Rorschach)

Disparagement of maternal figures:

Bony chest content; flat- or small-bosomed woman. (Schafer-Rorschach)

Disparagement of men:

Boys or "little boys" content, female subject; clown content; "dandies" content; dunces content; dwarf content; emphasis on short arms on male figures, female subject; gnome content; gremlin content; leprechaun; male puppet; man with no chin or receding-chin content; midget content; Pinnochio content. (Schafer-Rorschach)

Disparagement of men with fear of them:

D1 popular of III as animals. (Schafer-Rorschach)

Distrust of others: — Hole content. (Phillips and Smith)

Disturbance in mother–child relation: — Delay, evasion, Card VII. (Klopfer-Davidson)

Domination by father with concomitant constriction, inhibition of aggression, and lack of motivation for achievement: — Dimunitives (calf, colt, kitten, lamb, mouse, etc.). [Phillips and Smith]

Domination by father, with concomitant inhibition of aggression and lack of motivation for achievement: — Pup content; teddy bear content; toy dog; worm content; calf content; cub content; snail content. (Phillips and Smith)

Domineering, overprotective, possessive maternal figure: — Octopus content; scarab content; scorpion content; spider content. (Phillips and Smith)

Egocentric withdrawal: — Decrement A, M, P, possibly with overemphasis on certain content categories. (Beck III)

Emotional responsivity with self-control: — FC. (Phillips and Smith)

Fear of hostility of others: — Tiger content. (Phillips and Smith)

Fear of injury from others: — Hd limbs (legs and arms) content. (Phillips and Smith)

Fear of punitive reactions from others: — Complimentary remarks about cards. (Phillips and Smith)

Fear of rejection: — Shading twice the number of color responses. (Klopfer-Developments I)

Fear in men of women: — Spinal cord and spine content. (Phillips and Smith)

Feeling of abandonment: — Canyon, chasm, cliff content. (Phillips and Smith)

Feeling of anxiety and of vulnerability with paternal figure: — Giant threatening figure on Card IV. (Schafer-Rorschach)

Feeling of inadequacy relative to success of father: — Bridge content. (Phillips and Smith)

Feeling of isolation from others: — Barren and deserted places; desert content; little-island content (Schafer-Rorschach); cold objects and scenes

	(ice, snow, etc.); vista landscapes, especially islands (Beck and Molish); desolate landscapes (swamps, etc.); island content; H seen at distance (Beck III); island content. (Phillips and Smith)
Feelings of rejection:	Canyon content; island content (Phillips and Smith); chicken content. (Schafer-Rorschach)
Felt inferior social status:	Ragged or torn objects. (Schafer-Rorschach)
Inept social behavior:	Hd other than faces and heads. (Klopfer-Developments I)
Lack of interest in social exchange:	Mumbling. (Phillips and Smith)
Female: relationship with punitive or weak contemporary male with depression and anxiety:	Edging, shock, Card III. (Phillips and Smith)
Friendly, responsive:	Carnival content; clown content; dance content; embrace content; frolic content; kissing content; snuggling content; toy content. (Schafer-Rorschach)
Good interpersonal relations with self-acceptance:	M+. (Klopfer-Davidson)
Guarded interpersonal relations:	Anemometer; governor on steam engine; shell content; walls content. (Schafer-Rorschach)
Hostile, disparaging attitude toward males:	"Trained elephants performing an act" content, female subject. (Schafer-Rorschach)
Hostile view of male as implicitly inert and passive:	Sleeping males, female subject. (Schafer-Rorschach)
Hostility toward that figure:	Headless figure. (Beck III)
Hostility toward maternal figure:	Headless woman; witch content. (Beck III)
Hostility toward women:	Witch content. (Beck and Molish)
Impaired relationship with female figures:	Absence female H. (Klopfer-Developments I)

Impaired relationship with maternal figure:	Human popular elsewhere, no human popular on VII. (Klopfer-Developments I)
Impaired relationship with paternal figure:	Absence male H. (Klopfer-Developments I)
Impersonal relationships:	Authoritative, supernatural or threatening figures; automaton content; elevated or low social status symbols; servant content; symbols of rebellion and revolution. (Schafer-Rorschach)
Inability to sustain close relationships:	(H) content. (Klopfer-Davidson)
Indulgent maternal figure:	Cow content; deer content (Phillips and Smith); sheep content. (Klopfer-Davidson)
Infantile social behavior:	Card VIII popular human as animals or children. (Klopfer-Developments I)
Inimical maternal figure:	Witch content. (Klopfer-Davidson)
Insecurity with distrust of but desire for nurturing relationship:	Buildings and towers content. (Phillips and Smith)
Insecurity in interpersonal relationships:	Hole content; precision alternatives with first rejected for second. (Phillips and Smith)
Interpersonal relations important to subject; sensitivity to others:	Movement in full human content. (Phillips and Smith)
Interest in others and sensitivity to them:	Human content. (Phillips and Smith)
Isolation from others:	Map content. (Phillips and Smith)
Lack of empathy:	Decrement M (Klopfer-Davidson); Eskimo content (Schafer-Rorschach); no H content (Klopfer-Developments I); statement that blots do not suggest a response. (Phillips and Smith)
Lack of empathy with inability to identify with others:	Inability to perceive human popular, Card III. (Klopfer-Developments I)

Lack of need or indifference to need for affection, as in antisocial personality:	Indifference to shading. (Klopfer-Developments II)
Lack of responsivity:	R Cards VIII, IX, and X < 30%. (Klopfer-Developments I; Klopfer-Davidson)
Lack of responsivity to social pressure:	Absence of elaboration, avoidance of additional responses to cards, terse style. (Phillips and Smith)
Loneliness:	Barren and deserted places (Schafer-Rorschach); (Hd) content (Phillips and Smith); vista landscapes, especially islands. (Beck and Molish)
Male: harsh punitive paternal figure:	Edging, shock, Card III. (Phillips and Smith)
Manipulation of others for nurturance needs:	Food content. (Phillips and Smith)
Masochism possibly, with maternal figure conceived of as destructive:	Witch content. (Schafer-Rorschach)
Maternal figure conceived of as destructive:	Spider, witches. (Schafer-Rorschach)
Maternal overprotection:	Fish content. (Phillips and Smith)
Need for responsivity from others:	FT. (Klopfer-Davidson)
Need for social interaction:	FC+, FT+, M+. (Klopfer-Developments I)
Optimum social interaction:	Color > 2 X texture. (Klopfer-Davidson)
Persons resistant to social pressure:	Completely unmodified, unqualified, terse responses. (Phillips and Smith)
Potential for acceptable social adjustment:	Totem pole content. (Phillips and Smith)
Projection of feeling about people, as ugly, attractive, or menacing:	Perception of H in terms of attributes. (Klopfer-Davidson)
Punitive paternal figure:	Edging, shock, Card IV. (Phillips and Smith)

Rejecting maternal figure with concomitant anticipation of rejection, covert hostility, and heterosexual inadequacy:

Crab content; lobster content. (Phillips and Smith)

Rejection by maternal figure:

Ice, snow content. (Phillips and Smith)

Reluctant conformity to social pressures:

Preliminary remarks connoting hesitation. (Phillips and Smith)

Sensivity to and interest in others but with social anxiety:

(H) + 1. (Phillips and Smith)

Shallow affability:

Texture alone. (Phillips and Smith)

Sibling rivalry with absence of insight:

Gums and teeth content. (Phillips and Smith)

Sociability:

P. (Phillips and Smith)

Social anxiety:

Confabulation, W below expectancy; detailing; doubt expressed about adequacy of percept; exclusive FC; Hd content; M in Hd; M > WM; T, TF (Phillips and Smith); profile increment. (Klopfer-Davidson)

Social anxiety and constraint:

Non-P bony anatomy content. (Phillips and Smith)

Social anxiety with need for social interaction:

FC equal to C + CF. (Klopfer-Davidson)

Social anxiety and restriction with self-doubt and tension:

Cut-off W. (Phillips and Smith)

Social anxiety with self-consciousness perhaps and need for social approval:

Inappropriate color FC ("pink animals"). [Klopfer-Developments I]

Social anxiety with self-distrust:

Excessive prefatory remarks and qualification. (Phillips and Smith)

Social anxiety; withdrawal for fear of rejection:

Texture 2 X color. (Klopfer-Davidson)

Social dependence:

Increment FC. (Klopfer-Developments I)

Social graces without spontaneous emotional involvement:

Decrement or no CF; increment FC. (Klopfer-Developments I)

Social isolation:

Absence of popular as first response, Card I; C + CF > FC; elaboration below expectancy; F% above expectancy; H below expectancy; (Hd) content; R below expectancy. (Phillips and Smith)

Social maladjustment if intelligence is average or above average:

Smoke content. (Phillips and Smith)

Social responsivity:

FC. (Beck and Molish)

Superficiality in social relations:

FC > CF; FC only or almost exclusively. (Klopfer-Davidson)

Uncertainty in regard to social role:

Perplexity. (Phillips and Smith)

Unfriendly, unresponsive:

Ice content; iceberg content; polar bear content; snow content. (Schafer-Rorschach)

Unresolved relationship with paternal figure viewed as domineering but sympathetic:

Bear content. (Phillips and Smith)

Unstable interpersonal relationships:

Comment on inquiry that blot no longer appears like original percept. (Phillips and Smith)

Rorschach Stimuli and Response

Absent unless depression is reactive or passive-dependent character is ambivalent:

Space in depressive and passive-dependent states. (Beck and Molish)

Attempt to restructure the situation by establishing rules:

Inquiry by subject in regard to how he is expected to perform. (Phillips and Smith)

Avoidance of red areas:

Avoidance of emotionality. (Schafer-Rorschach)

Card III:

Unlikely to elicit shock. (Beck and Molish)

Cards II and III about equally; VIII, X:

Cards most likely to elicit color shock. (Beck and Molish)

Cards IV, VI, VII about equally, followed by V and I:

Cards most likely to elicit shading shock. (Beck and Molish)

Color dominance over form:

H below expectancy. (Phillips and Smith)

Common on Card I in paranoid
syndromes:

Eagle content. (Phillips and Smith)

Curiosity:

Looking at back of cards. (Phillips
and Smith)

Decreases with psychosis, increases
with anxiety:

F+. (Phillips and Smith)

Delayed response:

Diminutive, passive, or plodding animals. (Schafer-Rorschach)

Effort to make a game of Rorschach
testing; it's not to be taken seriously:

Facetious closing remarks to terminate
card responses. (Schafer-Rorschach)

Especially likely to evoke texture
responses:

Card IV. (Beck and Molish)

Form dominance over color:

H equal to or above expectancy.
(Phillips and Smith)

Greater anxiety than when this
occurs on IV, VI, and VII:

F– and shading responses, II, III, V.
(Rapaport)

Manifest anxiety; may be greater
for cards relating to conflict areas:

Excessive unsystematic turning uninterrupted by interpretations.
(Phillips and Smith)

May be evoked by association a
particular card suggests:

Rejections. (Schafer-Rorschach)

May be indicative of shock:

Response time 40″ or more.
(Phillips and Smith)

May symbolize primitive impulses:

Primitive people content. (Schafer-
Rorschach)

May symbolize primitive hostile
impulses:

Dinosaur content. (Schafer-Rorschach)

Shock indicative of anxiety:

Most prevalent on Cards IV, VI, VII.
(Beck III)

Reflects patient's attitude, mood,
and self-conception:

Facial expression. (Rapaport)

Shock; card represents conflict area
and turning is avoidance:

Nonconsistent immediate turning of
card. (Phillips and Smith)

Symbolizes children:

Small animal content. (Phillips and
Smith)

Symbolize parents:

Large A. (Phillips and Smith)

Thirty seconds (30"):

Optimum reaction time. (Klopfer-Davidson)

Sexual Function and Role

Aberrant sex practices:

Edging, shock, Card VI (tends to be shock on III as well with aberrant sex practices). [Phillips and Smith]

Ambiguous sexual role:

Nonderogatory remarks about grotesque or strange appearance of the cards. (Phillips and Smith)

Anality:

Anal associations (anus, rectum, colon, etc.); animal and people rear-view content; animal or person defecating content; back-to-back posture of animals and humans; bustle content; buttocks content; buttocks bumping or touching; dirt and mess associations; feces content; figures seen from behind or with backs turned; gas mask content; mud content; persons back to back; reference to exhaust systems of machinery; smear content; splatter content; squatting posture; stain content; toilet seat content. (Schafer-Rorschach)

Anality possibly:

Hole content. (Schafer-Rorschach)

Analysands, associates of the examiner, self-consciously nonconformist subject:

Sex content. (Phillips and Smith)

Anticipation, anxiety, and curiosity regarding reproduction:

Ovary content at child-bearing age. (Schafer-Rorschach)

Anxiety possibly over sexual curiosity and impulses:

Shock on Cards II and VII, female subject. (Beck and Molish)

Birth associations:

Flower bud. (Schafer-Rorschach)

Cards II, VII, IX; heterosexual anxiety:

White space shock. (Beck and Molish)

Castration anxiety:

Scarecrow content; straw man content. (Schafer-Rorschach)

Castration anxiety in men:	Scars and wounds content. (Schafer-Rorschach)
Castration anxiety in men, castration feelings in women:	Blind or missing eyes; cut content; nutcracker content; pliers content; tree stump content; tweezers content; truss content; unfinished figures content. (Schafer-Rorschach)
Castration anxiety possibly; concern over body integrity:	Dead, missing, or mutilated animal, human, and plant limbs; missing parts content; ragged and torn animal skins content; tattered and torn butterflies content. (Schafer-Rorschach)
Castration anxiety; possible fear of injury:	Shock on Card VI, male subjects. (Beck and Molish)
Castration (emasculation) complex conflict possibly:	Artificial or missing biting or punching surfaces (false teeth, toothless face); little devouring or attacking animals (minature dragons, mosquitoes). [Schafer-Rorschach]
Castration fantasies or fears:	Body mutilation. (Schafer-Rorschach)
Castration (emasculation) fears and wishes; feminine trend in men, masculine trend in women:	Anxiety over death, killing, and mutilation responses. (Schafer-Rorschach)
Castration feelings and masculine identification in women:	Scars and wounds content. (Schafer-Rorschach)
Castration (emasculation) impulses:	Emphasis on short arms on male figures, female subjects. (Schafer-Rorschach)
Childhood fantasy concept of heterosexual relationships; conception of females as innocent, sexually repressed, and indulged by gallant and depreciated males:	Snow White and the seven dwarfs. (Schafer-Rorschach)
Competitive woman in involutional period:	Spinal cord and spine content. (Phillips and Smith)
Concern with childlessness or loss of reproductive function in women:	Desert content. (Schafer-Rorschach)

Concern over loss of maternal role:	Ovary content at end of child-bearing age (after or near menopause). [Schafer-Rorschach]
Concern with reproductive function:	Botanical parts and reproductive anatomy; childbirth associations; deteriorated or dilapidated pelvic anatomy; egg content; embryo, fetus; emphasis on internal space associations; flower-bud content. (Schafer-Rorschach)
Concern over sexual role:	Clothing content. (Phillips and Smith)
Concern with reproductive function:	Ovary content; pistil content; pollen content; pregnant or swollen abdomen; seed content; semen content; stamen content; stork content; swollen or pregnant abdomen; umbilical cord content; uterus content; woman in delivery position; womb content. (Schafer-Rorschach)
Conflicted or inadequate heterosexual relations:	Edging, shock, Card VII. (Phillips and Smith)
Defense against masculine penetration:	Dragons at the entrance to a building; gargoyles over a doorway. (Schafer-Rorschach)
Denial of sensuality needs possibly:	Avoidance of shading or emphasis only on light rather than heavy shading. (Schafer-Rorschach)
Denial of sexual inadequacy or ineffectuality:	Genitalia increment. (Klopfer-Developments I)
Difficulty with the male role:	Avoidance of projection, Card VI, male subject. (Klopfer-Davidson)
Disparagement of men; feminine inadequacy and masculine identification:	Andy Gump; artificial or missing antlers on a deer. (Schafer-Rorschach)
Failure of man in heterosexual relationship:	Snail content; worm content. (Phillips and Smith)
Fear or feeling of loss of masculinity possibly:	Damaged or impaired objects, male subjects. (Schafer-Rorschach)
Fearful, hostile conception of male role:	Bleeding hymen content. (Schafer-Rorschach)

Fear of inadequate masculinity; possible associated difficulty in experiencing tender affection in relationship with females:

Disparaging of female sexual organ percepts, male subject. (Schafer-Rorschach)

Feeling of decline or loss of reproductive function with advancing age:

Old-plant content. (Schafer-Rorschach)

Female subject: competitiveness toward and disparagement of men; male subject; feeling of masculine inadequacy:

Incomplete or small male figure. (Schafer-Rorschach)

Female: traumatic heterosexual problems:

Edging, shock, Card III. (Phillips and Smith)

Feminine attitudes and interests (feminine tendency or traits):

Art content; personal content. (Phillips and Smith)

Feminine attributes in men; sexual role conflict possibly:

FT and FY increment (Beck and Molish); H carrying basket. (Klopfer-Developments I)

Feminine identification in men:

Animal or person defecating content; awkward or missing wings on birds content (birds without wings); badly baked cookie; badly tied bow tie; birth and reproductive images and organs content; bed jacket content; bleeding rectum content; bleeding vagina content; body without backbone; bustle content; buttocks content; buttocks bumping or touching content; candelabra content; centaur content; charging bull content; corset content; cosmetics content; creature with talons around anus content; crudely skinned animal; dangling legs content; demon content; devastating fires content; dirt associations; drooping arms; dunce cap; feces content; figure seen from behind or with back turned; flaming tail of jet plane or rocket; gas mask; gossip content; gown content; hatchet content; horns content; jellyfish content; jewelry content; King Kong content; Ku Klux Klan figure content; mice barely hanging on; mud content; "old hen" (woman) content; perfume bottle content; persons back to back content; pregnancy content; pretty flowers content; Prussian content; rear end of animals content; rhinoceros content; rifle content; savages content; saw content; scarecrow content; scars and wounds content; shears content; silk content; smear content; smeared slide; spear content; stain content; stinger content; stockings content; straw man content; taffeta content; toilet seat content; vase content; web content; wings too heavy or large for body. (Schafer-Rorschach)

Feminine identification with fear of women:

Amazon content; Medusa content; shrew content; witch content. (Schafer-Rorschach)

Feminine identification in men, masculine identification in women:

Anal associations (anus, rectum, colon, etc.); apeman content; athletic or mechanical associations with masculine connotations; bestiality content; biting animals content, with increment other anal, oral, or sex content; blind or missing eyes content; blindness content; bludgeoning and penetrating tools and weapons; caveman content; club content; cat content; cutting and squeezing implements; dead branch content; dead, missing, or mutilated animal, human, and plant limbs; doubled-barreled shotgun; either or mixed sex; feminine adornments, garments, and objects; fighting cocks; gigantic penis; hostile designations for women; increment anal, oral, sexual associations (anus, breasts, colon, rectum; devouring animals, food, mouth; penis, sexual intercourse, testicles, vagina, womb); increment women engaged in feminine or passive activities; lesbians embracing; lower middle card I and upper middle card II as vagina; lower middle cards II and VII, upper middle IV as penis; man with cosmetics; men embracing; men in gowns, as mandarins or monks; middle figure of Card I as man; missing-parts content; popular figure on Card III as woman or bisexual; primitive aggressive males (apeman, caveman); reference to sexual deviation activities or figures; reversal of sex of figure or of sexual anatomy usually seen; scantily clad women; symmetrical figures identified as one sex on one side and the opposite sex on the other; trap content; tree stump; truss content; unfinished figures; vagina with hooks in it; weakness associations; web content; woman masturbating man. (Schafer-Rorschach)

Feminine inadequacy:

Baseball bat; bony chest; bowling pin content; boys or "little boys" content; "dandies" content; dragons at the entrance to a building; dunces content; dwarf content; flat- or small-bosomed woman; gargoyles over a doorway; gnome content; gremlin content; ice station; Little Lord Fauntleroy content; man with no chin or receding-chin content; menstrual or vaginal associations with revulsion; mountain climbers content; named mechanical objects, as wing of a DC-3; umpire content; vacuous

	looking woman; women engaged in trivial gossip. (Schafer-Rorschach)
Feminine and masculine inadequacy:	Apeman content; arrow content; bestiality content; biting animals content with increment anal, oral, or sexual content; bleeding hymen content; caveman content; club content; double-barreled shotgun content; fighting cocks content; lesbians embracing content; lower middle Card I and upper middle Card II as vagina; lower middle Cards II and VII, upper middle Card IV, as penis; men embracing; man with cosmetics; men in gowns, as mandarins or monks; middle figure of Card I as man; woman masturbating man. (Schafer-Rorschach)
Feminine and masculine inadequacy with negative attitudes:	Nutcracker content; truss content; tweezers content. (Schafer-Rorschach)
Feminine tendency:	Art content; botany content; esthetic forms (snowflakes, etc.); female for Card III popular; female figures on other than Card VII; music content; personal content; smooth texture (Phillips and Smith); soft FT. (Beck and Molish)
Guilt over sexual impulses and needs:	Area D11 of Card VII as church (Schafer-Rorschach); nonblatant religious content (priest, etc.). [Phillips and Smith]
Heterosexual anxiety with possible feminine identification:	Shock on Cards II and VII, male subject. (Beck and Molish)
Heterosexual conflict or homosexual anxiety:	Shock on Card VI. (Beck and Molish)
Heterosexual inadequacy:	Bird content; cockroach content; figure facing away from subject. (Phillips and Smith; Klopfer-Developments I)
Homosexual fears and wishes possibly:	Long nose. (Schafer-Rorschach)

Homosexual tendency (homosexual impulses, homosexuality):

Cartoon content; H perceived as double-sexed man or woman; perception of female where male is usually seen (other than Card III); statue content; uncertainty as to sex (other than Card III) [Phillips and Smith]; symmetrical females as male–female instead of same sex. (Rapaport)

Homosexual tendency possibly:

Anal content; art content; calf content; confusion or perplexity relative to sex of H; "dancing" H; displacing or penetrating Fm content; emphasis on sex content; flower and leaf content; (H) content; mythology content; seeing content usually perceived as one sex as the opposite sex (other than Card III); shock on cards III and VI; women's clothing content (Phillips and Smith); beard emphasis; hair emphasis; overemphasis on texture; perception of breast on D1 human, Card III (Beck and Molish); confusion of sexual characteristics; double-sex H; emphasis on sex organs or sex functions of animals; pans and satyrs possibly; reversal of sex of figure or of sexual anatomy usually seen (Beck III); lips and lipstick content (Schafer-Clinical Application, Schafer-Rorschach); "whirling" percepts. (Schafer-Clinical Application)

Homosexual tendency possibly, female subject:

Depreciation of H, especially male figures. (Beck and Molish)

Homosexual tendency possibly, with it a source of anxiety:

Severe shock, Card IV. (Beck and Molish)

Hostile disparagement of males, masculine identification in women:

Increment diminutive and disparaged male figures, or male figures in absurd or demeaning acts and postures, female subject. (Schafer-Rorschach)

Hostile, fearful conception of masculine role:

Double-barreled shotgun. (Schafer-Rorschach)

Impotency (impotence):

Awkward and missing wings on birds (birds without wings); badly baked cookie; badly tied bowtie; body without backbone; botched or poorly prepared adornments, materials, and specimens; crudely skinned animal; drooping or limp limbs and organisms; helpless, powerless animals or figures; loss of grip associations; scarecrow content; smeared slide; straw man content; wings too large or heavy for body. (Schafer-Rorschach)

In female subject may represent masculine striving:

Horns content. (Schafer-Rorschach)

In male subject sexual role conflict, possible lack of masculine identification:

Lack of W to Card IV, W's elsewhere. (Klopfer-Developments I)

Instability in sexual relationship:

Precision alternatives with first rejected for second. (Phillips and Smith)

In women concern over childlessness, frigidity, and/or loss of reproductive capacity:

Ice formation in cave. (Schafer-Rorschach)

Lack of sexual aggressiveness:

Mouse (with tail). [Klopfer-Davidson]

Male: economic and psychosexual maladjustment (exhibitionism, homosexuality):

Edging, shock, Card III. (Phillips and Smith)

Masculine activity, possibly compensatory:

Implement content. (Phillips and Smith)

Masculine identification:

Buildings and towers content. (Phillips and Smith)

Masculine identification in women:

Barriers (dragons at entrance of building, gargoyles over doorway, shield); baseball bat; belittling of conventional feminine activity or female figures; bleeding vagina content;

bony chest; bowling pin content; boys or "little boys" content, female subject; "dandies" content; dunces content; dwarf content; flat- or small-bosomed woman; gnome content; gremlin content; ice skates content; Little Lord Fauntleroy content; man with no chin or receding chin content; mountain climbers content; named mechanical objects, as wings of DC-3; negative associations having to do with menstrual or vaginal function; sensuous emphasis on appearance of female figures; umpire content; vacuous-looking woman content. (Schafer-Rorschach)

Masculine identification in women; rejection of feminine role:

Menstrual or vaginal associations with revulsion; woman engaged in trivial gossip. (Schafer-Rorschach)

Masculine inadequacy:

Amazon content; animal or person defecating content; athletic or mechanical associations with masculine connotations; awkward or missing wings on birds; bed jacket content; bleeding rectum content; bludgeoning and penetrating tools and weapons; body without backbone; bustle content; buttocks content; buttocks bumping or touching content; candelabra content; centaur content; charging bull; corset content; cosmetics content; creature with talons around anus; crudely skinned animal content; cutting or squeezing implement content; dead, missing, or mutilated animal or human limbs; demon content; devastating fires content; dirt associations; dunce cap; either or mixed sex; feces content; feminine adornments, garments, and objects;

figures seen from behind or with backs turned; flaming tail of jet plane or rocket; gown content; hatchet content; horns content; hostile designations for women; increment anal, oral, sexual associations (anus, colon, rectum; devouring animals, food, mouth; breasts, penis, sexual intercourse, testicles, vagina, womb); increment women engaged in feminine or passive activities; jellyfish content; jewelry content; King Kong content; Ku Klux Klan figures content; Medusa content; mice barely holding on; missing-part content; mud content; "old hen" (woman) content; perfume bottle; persons back to back; pliers content; pregnancy content; pretty flowers; primitive aggressive males (apeman, caveman); rear end of animals; reference to sexual deviation activities or figures; reversal of sex of figure and of sexual anatomy usually seen; rhinoceros content; rifle content; savages content; saw content; scantily clad women; scarecrow content; scars and wounds content; shears content; shrew content; silk content; smear content; smeared slide; spear content; stain content; stinger content; stockings content; straw man content; taffeta content; toilet seat content; trap content; vagina with hooks in it content; vase content; vocation content; weakness associations; web content; wings too large or heavy for body; witch content. (Schafer-Rorschach)

Masculine striving:

Architecture content, female subject. (Rapaport)

Masculinity, perhaps compensatory for feelings of inadequacy:	Vocation content. (Phillips and Smith)
Masculinity (in women subjects suggests a homosexual potential):	Extensor M. (Beck and Molish; Beck III)
Masturbation guilt with absence of insight:	Gums and teeth content. (Phillips and Smith)
May suggest feminine identification (male subjects):	Feminine undergarments content. (Phillips and Smith)
May symbolize passive-receptive feminine trend—literally female genitalia:	House with hedge. (Schafer-Rorschach)
Oedipal conflicts possibly:	Birth and reproductive images and organs content, male subject. (Schafer-Rorschach)
Oedipal complex possibly:	Shading shock, cards IV and VII. (Beck and Molish)
Oral-eroticism:	Figure-kissing content; lips content; lipstick content. (Schafer-Rorschach)
Oral-erotic and passive-receptive tendency:	Kissing and lip associations. (Schafer-Rorschach)
Passive-feminine tendency:	Butterfly (nonpopular); snail content; teddy bear content; toy dog content. (Phillips and Smith)
Passive-feminine, possible homosexual tendency:	Calf content; cub content; diminutives (calf, colt, kitten, lamb, mouse, etc.); pup content; worm content. (Phillips and Smith)
Passive-feminine submissive tendency (including in male subjects, where it suggests a homosexual potential):	Flexor M. (Beck and Molish)
Phallic symbol possibly:	Long nose. (Schafer-Rorschach)
Potential for mature sexual relationships:	Form-plus response to top projection, Card VI. (Klopfer-Developments I)
Pregenital sex fixations:	Genitalia increment. (Klopfer-Developments I)

Rejecting maternal figure with concomitant heterosexual inadequacy:

Bug (beetle) content.   (Phillips and Smith)

Rejection of intimacy possibly, including in the sexual relationship:

Eskimo content. (Schafer-Rorschach)

Rejection of women as sexual objects possibly:

Rejection female P, Card VII. (Beck and Molish)

Seductiveness and possible promiscuity as a way of relating to others:

Exhibitionistic display of sexual areas by dress and posture; flirtatiousness. (Schafer-Rorschach)

Sensuality:

Adornment associations and objects; clothing content; dress-form content; exotic associations with the Arabian Nights; hairdresser's headrest; jewelry content; nude or scantily dressed women (chorus girl, sunbather); peacock content; perfume bottle content (Schafer-Rorschach); TF. (Klopfer-Davidson)

Sensuality possibly:

FT. (Beck and Molish)

Sexual conflict:

Avoidance of projection, F– content, Card VI (Klopfer-Developments I); visceral anatomy content. (Rapaport)

Sexual conflict and guilt possibly:

Bed linen hung out to dry content. (Schafer-Rorschach)

Sexual identification conflict:

"Bending over" content (Phillips and Smith); H called "persons." (Klopfer-Developments I)

Sexual identification conflict; bisexuality:

"Person" content. (Phillips and Smith)

Sexual inadequacy in men:

Lake, river, stream content. (Phillips and Smith)

Sexual inhibition and repression:

Area D11 of Card VII as church. (Schafer-Rorschach)

Sexual maladjustment:

Anal content.   (Phillips and Smith)

Sexual preoccupation:

Hysterical features with usual sex content; lips content; lipstick content;

sex response to Card I (Schafer-Clinical Application); increment responses to projection area of Card VI, not necessarily overtly sexual in content (Klopfer-Developments I); sex content. (Rapaport)

Sexual preoccupation with socially acceptable expression:

Sexually aggressive (H) (as satyr); thinly clad H (showgirl). [Phillips and Smith]

Sexually preoccupied analysand:

Many nondeviant sex responses. (Schafer-Clinical Application)

Sexual role conflict:

Center D popular, Card I, seen from rear or as cloaked; female in masculine activity or role (Klopfer-Developments I); "strange appearance" fabulization. (Phillips and Smith)

Sexual symbolism:

House content; snake (and other named snake species); totem pole content. (Klopfer-Davidson)

Skin eroticism:

Stroking or touching cards. (Phillips and Smith)

Some homosexuals:

Low P. (Beck III)

Uncertainty in regard to sexual role:

Perplexity. (Phillips and Smith)

Unsuccessful heterosexuality:

Edging, shock, Card VI. (Phillips and Smith)

Voyeuristic tendency:

Peering, staring content (Beck III); stated inability to produce a response. (Phillips and Smith)

Weakness in men:

Crudely skinned animal; mice barely hanging on.   (Schafer-Rorschach)

With anal, oral, and sexual content, masculine or feminine inadequacy:

Animals devouring other animals or persons. (Schafer-Rorschach)

With increment anal, oral, and sexual content, feminine masculine inadequacy—feminine identification in men, masculine identification in women:

Clawing animals. (Schafer-Rorschach)

With increment other anal, oral, sexual content, masculine and feminine inadequacy—feminine identification in men:

Pursuing animals. (Schafer-Rorschach)

Women:

Personal content. (Phillips and Smith)

Women: sexual apprehension and inadequacy:

Edging, shock, Card IV. (Phillips and Smith)

Situational States

Concern over advancing age:

Flower-bud content. (Schafer-Rorschach)

Concern with aging and death:

Bleeding leg content; bleeding vagina content; bombed building; damaged, deteriorated, diseased, or frayed anatomy, objects, and plants; eroded pelvis content; falling bird shot in flight; frayed garment content; gangrenous tissue content; headless woman content; inflamed tissue; mangled wings; mangy fur; mummy content; old post; peg-leg sailor content; person being torn in half content; pus content; ragged boat; ruffle content; ruined wall; Shangri-la content; skull split open content; squashed tomcat content; stagnant water content; tattered clothes content; withered leaves content; worn-out skin content. (Schafer-Rorschach)

Deprivation feelings:

Desert content (Schafer-Rorschach); island content. (Phillips and Smith)

Feeling of decline:

Ovary content at end of child-bearing age (after or near menopause). [Schafer-Rorschach]

Low socioeconomic level:

Crude euphemisms, swearing, "yeah"; incorrect grammar. (Phillips and Smith)

People in trouble with the law:

Completely unmodified, unqualified, terse responses. (Phillips and Smith)

Reactive depression:

Color shock in depression (Beck and Molish); H equal to or less than Hd (Phillips and Smith); two or more form-plus M in depressive state. (Schafer-Clinical Application)

Symptomatology

Aggressive conflicts:

Visceral anatomy content. (Rapaport)

Anahedonism; lack of capacity for pleasurable experience:

Increment F+ (Beck III); no color. (Beck and Molish)

Anxiety:

(A+H)< 1/2 (Ad + Hd); Dd (edge details); anatomy, visceral; T, V, Y (Klopfer-Davidson); Adx + Hdx; A increment (declining M); card description; death content; F% and F+% above expectancy, with elaboration and R below expectancy; emblem content; excessive detailing; fabulization; Fm; frightening appearance fabulization; haphazard turning; high A%; high F+ with high P; hostile-environment comments; Hd content; increment At content; increment D; increment F+; increment (H), low M%, M in Hd; mutilation content; pedantically (but not peculiarly) worded anatomy; P beyond expectancy; reduction of H; reduction of M; reduction of R; W below expectancy; X-ray content (Phillips and Smith); blood content (Beck and Molish; Schafer-Rorschach); Card I as face (cat, jack o'lantern); decrement A + H; increment Ad + Hd; FM; interior D as clouds, Card I; turning, few or no responses with card turned (Klopfer-Developments I); CF, TF, YF increment; low F%; cloud content; devil content; questioning of own response (Schafer-Rorschach); color shock; constant speech (Beck and Molish); decrement D; decrement M; Hd content; increment Dd; long reaction time; W:D ratio 1:2 (Rapaport); decrement P; delayed reaction time; delayed reaction for first response; increment A; increment card turning; reduction in productivity (reduction in R); rejections; shading shock (Beck III); fire; Hdx; internal anatomy; TF, VF, YF (Beck and Molish); injury content (Beck and Molish; Phillips and Smith); low F% in constricted record; hysterical features with low F+; thunderstorm content.   (Schafer-Rorschach)

Anxiety, acute:

Adx and Hdx content. (Phillips and Smith)

Anxiety over aggressive impulses:

Refusal to hold cards. (Phillips and Smith)

Anxiety, often evoked by associations a particular card suggests:

Delayed reaction time and/or expression of uncertainty and inadequacy feelings. (Schafer-Rorschach)

Anxiety relative to dependency needs:

Fm in conjunction with or following FT. (Klopfer-Davidson)

Anxiety, diffuse:

TF, YF. (Schafer-Rorschach)

Anxiety, free-floating:

Cloud content; smoke content (Rapaport); Y (Beck and Molish; Rapaport); Y and YF (Schafer-Clinical Application)

Anxiety over hostility:

Avoidance of red areas.   (Schafer-Rorschach)

Anxiety over impulsivity, at conscious level:

Fm following or in blends with CF. (Klopfer-Developments I)

Anxiety, latent:

X-ray content. (Beck III)

Anxiety over loss of intellectual control possibly:

Headless figure. (Schafer-Rorschach)

Anxiety manifest:	Enumeration of parts; turning beyond normal expectancy (Phillips and Smith); T, TF. (Schafer-Rorschach)
Anxiety marked, possibly:	C, CF. (Beck and Molish; Schafer-Rorschach)
Anxiety, mild to moderate:	FY. (Phillips and Smith)
Anxiety, morbid:	Dropping or throwing a card to table with expression of fright or repulsion. (Phillips and Smith)
Anxiety, obsessive:	Card description. (Phillips and Smith)
Anxiety, paralyzing, in certain conflictful situations:	Increment pure Y. (Rapaport)
Anxiety, possibly:	Decrement R, W to D ratio 2:1. (Rapaport)
Anxiety, potential reducing:	FM + Fm> 1 1/2 M. (Klopfer-Davidson)
Anxiety over repressed hostility:	Bony anatomy content. (Phillips and Smith)
Anxiety, strong, inhibiting:	X-ray content. (Phillips and Smith)
Apathy:	Lackadaisical comments on mild disparity between response and blot outline. (Phillips and Smith)
A provocative act:	Tossing back card. (Phillips and Smith)
Apprehension (fearfulness):	"Bat coming toward me"; dark cave; dog scampering away; Dracula content; dragon content; enumeration of parts; fleeing dog; ghost content; gorilla content; monster content; protected animals like porcupine; protective clothing; sheltering terrain (Schafer-Rorschach); excessive prefatory remarks and qualifications; Hd content; missing-parts comment; more than two faces; nonderogatory remarks about the grotesque or strange appearance of the cards; shading shock; "strange appearance" fabulization

	(Phillips and Smith); eyes content; excessive qualification (Beck III); frightening creatures fabulization; interior Dd as clouds, Card I. (Klopfer-Developments I)
Apprehension if intelligence is average or above average:	Smoke content. (Phillips and Smith)
Apprehension marked:	X-ray content. (Phillips and Smith)
Apprehension; morbid anticipation of unpleasantness:	Non-P bat. (Phillips and Smith)
Caution:	Excessive prefatory remarks and qualification. (Phillips and Smith)
Conflict:	Fm. (Beck and Molish, citing Klein and Schlesinger)
Conflict areas:	Redundancy, superfluous elaboration (Phillips and Smith); F+ and F-, RT and other determinants in relation to particular cards (Klopfer-Davidson); slow response time. (Beck and Molish)
Conflict and tension with insight:	FM. (Klopfer-Davidson)
Decompensation fear or tendency:	Falling animals or humans. (Schafer-Rorschach)
Destructive impulses that are not acted out directly because of fear of retaliation:	Anatomy content. (Phillips and Smith)
Enuretics:	Crab content; fire content; frog content; jellyfish content; lobster content; octopus content; seahorse content; snail content; turtle content. (Phillips and Smith)
Expansiveness, grandiosity:	High W% with schizophrenic disorganization. (Schafer-Clinical Application)
Feeling of constriction:	Desert content. (Schafer-Rorschach)
Feeling of decay or deterioration:	Crumbled walls, toothless old man, withered leaf, worn-out rug. (Schafer-Rorschach)

Feeling of inadequacy (inferiority feelings, self-devaluation):	Architecture content; excessive qualification; increment qualifications, including question form of response (Beck III); decrement M; sheep content (Klopfer-Davidson); emblem content; mountain content; peculiar and pedantic prefatory remarks; rabbit content (Phillips and Smith); increment S, introversive experience balance (Klopfer-Developments I); use of phrase "*trying* to lift something" on card III P (Schafer-Clinical Application); vista. (Beck and Molish; Beck III)
Feeling of inadequacy relative to intellectual ability possibly:	Anatomy content (Beck and Molish); geography and science content (Beck and Molish; Klopfer-Davidson)
Feeling of inadequacy and lack of worth:	TF, VF, YF. (Beck and Molish)
Feelings of inadequacy possibly:	Distorted or mutilated animals and humans; emphasis on "big feet" of D2 area of Card IV. (Schafer-Rorschach)
Feelings of inadequacy which are projected possibly:	Criticism of blot. (Schafer-Rorschach)
Feelings of personal inadequacy:	Map with vista element, as aerial map. (Phillips and Smith)
Felt weakness:	Botched or poorly prepared adornments, materials, and specimens; drooping or limp limbs amd organisms; helpless, powerless animals or figures. (Schafer-Rorschach)
Felt weakness with anxiety:	Fleeing, frightening, and sinister animals, figures, and places. (Schafer-Rorschach)
Felt weakness with need for support and guidance:	Beacons, guiding beams, lighthouses, supporting objects. (Schafer-Rorschach)

Frustrated dependency:

Figure facing away from subject; mouth content. (Phillips and Smith)

Frustrated dependency with resentment:

Map content. (Phillips and Smith)

Guilt:

Dysphoric content; high A%; increment qualification, including question form of response; rigid sequence, self-depreciation; shading shock; hellfire and brimstone content; person on a rack. (Schafer-Rorschach)

Guilt over rebellious impulses:

Nonblatant religious H content (priest, etc.). [Phillips and Smith]

Helplessness:

"Bat coming toward me"; dark cave; dog scampering away; Dracula content; dragon content; fleeing dog; ghost content; gorilla content; monster content. (Schafer-Rorschach)

Hostility directed inward, with dysphoric mood, oppressive anxiety, and tension:

Increment M with space increment. (Beck and Molish)

Hypersensitivity:

CF. (Beck and Molish)

Impaired adjustment due to excessive dependence on others:

FT-. (Klopfer-Developments I)

Impaired ego strength:

M-. (Klopfer-Davidson)

Impaired or inadequate judgment:

Excessive rejections (Phillips and Smith); F- (Beck and Molish; Phillips and Smith)

Inability to concentrate:

Low F+. (Beck and Molish)

Inhibition of motility:

FY. (Phillips and Smith)

Insecurity:

"Base" percept (Schafer-Rorschach); canyon, chasm, cliff; clouds content; high F+ (with high R); high P; hostile-environment comments; "you" forms (Phillips and Smith); Card I as face (cat, jack-o-lantern); excluding parts of popular, Card I (Klopfer-Developments I); increment D. (Rapaport)

Lack of drive:	Low color. (Beck and Molish)
Lack of insight:	A>50%. (Phillips and Smith)
Lack of self-confidence:	Apologetic attitude; overqualification; redundancy. (Beck III)
Lack of self-esteem:	Derogatory self-references; remarks suggesting feeling of resignation over inability to produce response or further responses (Phillips and Smith); vulture content (Schafer-Rorschach); Y with shading shock. (Beck and Molish)
Maladjustment (chronic maladaptive behavior):	Extended F+ below 80% (Schafer-Rorschach); map content. (Phillips and Smith)
Mental inertia:	Decrement S, increment A and shading. (Beck III)
Negative prognostic sign:	Acute schizophrenic episode ("unclassified schizophrenia") with early disappearance FC (Schafer-Clinical Application); CF−; color naming; FC−; FM−; FT−; FY−; M−; T; TF; shading avoidance; shading denial (Klopfer-Developments I); Dd (edge details) [Rapaport]; DdM; M equals 3 × sum C; M in Hd (Phillips and Smith); experience balance of 0:0; low color and M in experience balance (coarctated EB) [Beck III]; indifference to shading. (Klopfer-Developments II)
Negative prognostic sign for therapy despite hysteric element:	Hysteria with anatomy and paranoid projection. (Beck and Molish)
Nihilistic fantasy probably:	Devastating fires, objects collapsing. (Beck III)
Passivity with anxiety:	Low color and M in experience balance (coarctated EB). [Beck III]
Pathology:	Alphabets, letters, and numerals content, adult subjects. (Klopfer-Davidson)

Perplexity:	Ambiequal experience balance, S increment. (Beck III)
Psychopathology:	Alphabets, letters, and numerals content, adult subjects (Klopfer-Davidson); color < M (Rapaport); inappropriate or strange vocalizations. (Phillips and Smith)
Psychopathology probably:	F-, Card I. (Phillips and Smith)
Request for reassurance:	Derogatory self-references. (Phillips and Smith)
Restlessness:	Color in conjunction with shading or vista (Beck III); increment Dd, without obsessive-compulsive features. (Schafer-Clinical Application)
Restless trend possibly:	Increment rotation, variability in productivity and time from card to card. (Beck III)
Self-criticality (self-devaluation):	Architecture content (Beck III); eagle content; excessive vista; perplexity (Phillips and Smith); increment S, introversive EB; Hd content; (H) content (Klopfer-Developments I); space with increment Dd, P, M (Rapaport); space in introversive setting. (Beck and Molish)
Self-doubt with self-consciousness:	Doubt expressed about adequacy of a percept. (Phillips and Smith)
Sense of nonfulfillment of self:	Vista architectural structures. (Beck and Molish)
Severe emotional disturbance:	Confused content, low F+, space. (Beck and Molish)
Shyness (timidity):	Card I as face (cat, jack-o-lantern) [Klopfer-Developments I] ; decrement color (Rapaport); diminutive, passive, or plodding animals; mask content; mouse content; snail content; turtle content (Schafer-Rorschach); rabbit content (Phillips and Smith; Schafer-

Rorschach); sheep content (Klopfer-Davidson)

Some disturbed schizophrenics and some epileptics of a nonchronic and undeteriorated kind:

Exceptionally low animal content. (Beck III)

Suggests inhibited motility:

Cool color preference; form dominance; M increment; shading. (Phillips and Smith)

Superego conflict:

Devil content; ears and eyes content; fire and hell content; helpless, powerless figures; Jehovah content; policeman content; religious figures and symbols; storybook animals and figures (good fairy, lamb) symbolic of innocence; symbols of law and morality. (Schafer-Rorschach)

Superego conflict with concern over morality:

Decalogue content; inquisition content; prophet content; Puritan content. (Schafer-Rorschach)

Superego conflict with guilt:

Black sheep content; cloven hoof content; hell associations; purgatory content; Satan content. (Schafer-Rorschach)

Superego, punitive:

Increment M with space increment. (Beck and Molish)

Tension (emotional tension):

Attention fluctuation, blocking, forgetting, inaccurate recall; color responses in conjunction with shading responses; excessive card turning; increment card turning; increment rotation, variation in productivity and time from card to card (Beck III); decrement color (Rapaport, Klopfer-Davidson); FM; increment FY; M > FM, FM<1/2M (Klopfer-Developments I); Fm. (Beck and Molish, citing Klein and Schlesinger)

Tension over impulse-control problem:

Powerful forces content (lightning, etc.). [Phillips and Smith]

Tension over repression of intense impulses pressing for expression:

Symmetry comments and responses. (Phillips and Smith)

Weak ego:

Decrement M and FM; mediocre or poor form. (Klopfer-Developments I)

Weakness:

Awkward or missing wings on birds (birds without wings); "bat coming toward me"; dark cave; dog scampering away; dragon content; drooping arms; fleeing dog; ghost content; gorilla content; monster content; scarecrow content. (Schafer-Rorschach)

Worry:

Increment FY. (Klopfer-Developments I)

Traits

Conforming passive-dependency, often with obsequiousness:

Increment P. (Beck III)

Delicacy:

Smooth texture. (Phillips and Smith)

Dependency (oral-dependency, passive-dependency):

Animals devouring other animals or persons; animals or persons arguing, spitting, sticking tongues out, yelling; asking for confirmation of adequacy of the response and for reassurance; Atlas content; baker content; big belly; biting animals; bird or nest content; brassiere content; breastplate content; camel content; cannibal content; carcass content; chicks with open beaks; Christmas stocking; Christmas tree content; clawing animals; claws content; cook content; cornucopia content; cow content; coyote content; crab content (other than popular D1, D7, and D8 of Card X); cradle content; crocodile content; decanter content; dentist's tools; Dracula content; eagle's beak;

emaciated face; false teeth; fangs content; fat-person content; feeding animals; fighting animals; figures kissing; flat- or small-bosomed woman; food content; frying pan content; good fairy content; hands raised in supplication; horseshoe content; jaws content; lamb content; lion content; lips content; lipstick content; man weighted down by pack; mosquito content; mother bird with worm; mother hen; mouth content; mouthless or toothless face; mule content; navel content; nipples content; nurse content; nursing lamb; ox content; person-eating content; person-praying content; person-sticking-tongue-out content; pig content; pit content; preying animals content; protective angel content; pursuing animals content; Santa Claus content; scarecrow content; shark content; skull of steer in desert content; sleeping infant; spider content; spider-web content; stomach content; syrup jar; table-setting content; tapeworm content; tattered figures content; throat content; tomato worm content; trap content; tusks content; umbilical cord content; vampire content; vise content; vulture content; waiter content; wasteland content; wild boar content; wishbone content, other than D3 on X; witch content; wolf content; woman with enveloping cloak content (Schafer-Rorschach); "any time limit?"; botany content; center detail increment (if M, insight is likely to be present into dependent needs); cloud content; emblem content; female figures on other than Card VII; fish

content; further inquiries about turning after permission is given; inquiry
as to whether it's permissible to turn
cards; lake, river, stream content;
preference for cool colors; questioning;
recreation content; smiling at examiner; spider content; tiger content
(Phillips and Smith); area D11 of
Card VII as house; soft Ft (Klopfer-
Developments I); breast content
(Klopfer-Developments I; Schafer-
Rorschach); flexor M (Beck and
Molish; Beck III); increment FT;
passive A, as cats, dogs, sheep; TF.
(Klopfer-Davidson)

Dependency, with associated feeling
of helplessness:

Upper inner D, Card I, as hands.
(Klopfer-Developments I)

Dependency of childish, inappropriate
degree:

Asking for confirmation of a response
("couldn't it?").   [Shafer-Clinical
Application]

Dependency of such degree as to
impair adjustment:

FT, FV, FY < T, TF, V, VF, Y.
(Klopfer-Davidson)

Dependency overwhelming:

FT + FY > ¾ F. (Klopfer-Davidson)

Dependency of parasitic degree:

Food content; larva, locusts, other
plant-devouring insects.
(Schafer-Rorschach)

Disinterest in trivia:

Decrement Dd. (Klopfer-Davidson)

Domestic interests:

Household content. (Beck III; Phillips
and Smith)

Eccentric element in personality:

Edging. (Beck III)

Egocentricity:

C + CF > FC; nonderogatory self-
references; "to me" prelude (Phillips
and Smith); emotional reaction to
response as reason why it was given;
self-references to justify response
(Schafer-Rorschach); Hd; (H); M approximately equal to FM, no color
(Klopfer-Developments I); pure C
(more than one). [Anderson-Beck]

Exactness, literality:	High F+. (Klopfer-Davidson)
Extratensiveness:	Color and texture (FT) [Klopfer-Developments I]; increment rotation; variability in productivity and time from card to card (Beck III); sum C > M. (Klopfer-Davidson)
Impotence:	Mice barely hanging on. (Schafer-Rorschach).
Impracticality:	Low P. (Beck III)
Impressionable suggestibility:	Pure C (more than one). [Rapaport]
Ineffectuality:	Lake, river, stream content. (Phillips and Smith)
Inertia (lethargy):	Affective range below 40 (Beck III); lying and sitting-down content; mask content; mouse content; rabbit content; resting content; sleeping content; sloth content; snail content; turtle content. (Schafer-Rorschach)
Ingratiation:	Complimentary remarks about cards. (Phillips and Smith)
Introspection (introversiveness, self-valuation, subjective reaction to environmental experience):	Abstraction content (Rapaport); animal and human movement, shading, vista (Klopfer-Developments I); kinesthetic responses (M) [Rorschach-Psychodianostics]; M > sum C (when M > 2 and color is at least one) [Klopfer-Davidson]; precision alternatives, vista (Phillips and Smith); low F%; vista reflection (mirrors, water surfaces). [Beck and Molish]
Introspective rumination:	Increment Dd. (Rapaport)
Irritability:	C, CF- (Beck and Molish); increment CF; F-; low-form color; rapid card turning; rapid speech; restlessness. (Beck III)
Lack of drive:	Decrement S, increment of A and shading. (Beck III)

Lack of initiative:

Jellyfish content. (Phillips and Smith)

Lack of perseverance:

$C + CF > FC$. (Phillips and Smith)

Lack of self-reliance:

"You" forms. (Phillips and Smith)

Lack of strong value system:

Decrement M. (Klopfer-Davidson)

Masochism; possible defeatist tendency:

Animal held down; bird shot in flight; bleeding, crushed, mutilated anatomy, animals and persons; bleeding leg; bombed building; burdened animals and people content; carnivorous animals and insects; damaged, deteriorated, diseased, or frayed animals, objects, persons, and plants; emaciated or tattered figures (beggar, scarecrow); eroded-pelvis content; falling bird shot in flight content; fire and hell content; gangrenous tissue content; headless woman content; hellfire and brimstone content; inflamed tissue content; mangled wings; mummy content; ox content; peg-leg sailor content; person on a rack content; pus content; ruined wall; rubble content; self-disparagement with rejection of reassurance, together with implicit provocation of rejection by examiner; shell-split-open content; slave content; squashed tomcat; stagnant water; tattered clothes; tattered figures content; withered leaves content (Schafer-Rorschach); skeletons, skulls content. (Klopfer-Developments I)

Masochism possibly:

Animals devouring other animals or persons; animals or persons arguing, spitting, sticking tongues out, yelling; Atlas content; biting animals; camel content; carcass content; clawing animals; coyote content; crab content (other than popular D1, D7, and D8 of Card IX; crocodile content; dentist's tools; Dracula content; fangs content; feeding animals; fighting animals; flat- or small-bosomed woman; man weighted down by pack; mouthless or toothless face; mule content; pit content; preying animals; pursuing animals; shark content; tapeworm content; teeth content; tiger content; tomato worm content; tattered persons content; vampire content; vice content; woman with enveloping cloak. (Schafer-Rorschach)

Meticulousness: Dd (edge details). [Phillips and Smith]

Naiveté: Botany or nature CF (Schafer-Clinical Application); emotional reaction to response as reason why it was given; perceiving cards as "evil" or "revolting"; loss of distance from percepts. (Schafer-Rorschach)

Narrow interests: A > 50%. (Klopfer-Davidson)

Overcompliance: Exclusive FC; pure C (more than one) [Phillips and Smith]; perseveration not produced by organic impairment. (Beck III)

Overcriticality: Wx (cut-off W). [Klopfer-Davidson]

Overemphasis on the obvious (mundane practicality):   Increment F + D (overemphasis on D). [Beck and Molish, Rapaport, Schafer-Rorschach]

Passivity (passive-receptive, passive-submissive):   Absence or marked decrement of space; excessive qualification; flexor stance; shading (Beck III); angel content; baker content; bed linen hung out to dry content; chicks with open beaks; Christmas associations; Christmas stocking; Christmas tree; cook content; cornucopia content; cow content; crushed or squashed figure; decanter content; decline of R as test continues and complaints about demands of test or time it takes;

embryo, fetus; fat-person content; feeding animals; figure kissing; "floating" percepts (clouds etc.); food associations (feed, food service, food utensils, etc.); frying pan content; good fairy content; good luck symbols (horseshoe, wishbone); hands raised in supplication; increment A + P; increment FC; inert states (sloth, snail); infant content; ingratiation followed by petulance as test continues; kissing content; lip associations (lips, lipstick, etc.); lying or sitting-down content; maternal animals or persons; mother bird with worm; mother hen content; mouth content; navel content; nipples content; nurse content; nursing lamb content; orchid content; person-eating content; person praying; pig content; prayer associations; religious protective figures, such as angels; "resting" content; Santa Claus content; sleeping content; stomach content; syrup jar content; table-setting content; throat content; umbilical cord content; water content; wishbone content, other than D3 on X (Schafer-Rorschach) "bending over" content; clouds content; covering parts of blot with hand to exclude non-percept area; emphasis on anal content; fire content; holding card after terminal remarks until examiner removes it; inquiry as to whether it is permissible to turn cards; overemphasis on inactive M; preliminary remarks connoting hesitation; remarks suggesting feeling of resignation over inability to produce response or further responses; remarks implying response source is intrinsic to blot or objects it resembles; response time 10" or less; stroking or touching cards; "suggests to me" (Phillips and Smith); cow content; sheep content (Klopfer-Developments I); FC only or main color (Schafer-Clinical Application); M equal to sum C (Klopfer-Davidson); TF, VF, YF. (Beck and Molish)

Restraint: Household content. (Phillips and Smith)

Suggestibility possibly: Position responses. (Beck and Molish)

Reflective or ruminative tendency possibly: M > color; M+. (Rapaport)

Strong oral needs: Food content. (Schafer-Clinical Application)

Unresponsive to conventional concepts: Low P. (Schafer-Clinical Application)

Suggestibility: Perseveration (not produced by organic impairment). [Beck III]

Superficiality: Color naming; FC increment, minimum or no C or CF. (Klopfer-Developments I)

Tact: FC. (Klopfer-Developments I)

BIBLIOGRAPHY

1. Beck, Samuel J., Beck, Anne G., Levitt, Eugene E., and Molish, Herman B.: *Rorschach's Test,* vol. 1, 3rd ed., New York, Grune, 1961; vol. II, *A Variety of Personality Pictures,* 2nd ed., with Molish, H. B. 1967 [Beck and Molish] ; and vol. III, *Advances in Interpretation,* 1952 [Beck III].
2. Beck, Samuel J.: The Rorschach test: A multi-dimensional test of personality. In Anderson, Harold H., and Anderson, G. L.: *An Introduction to Projective Techniques.* New York, Prentice-Hall, 1951 [Anderson-Beck].
3. Bender, Lauretta: *A Visual Motor Gestalt Test and its Clinical Use.* New York, American Orthopsychiatric Association, 1938 [Bender].
4. Gilbert, Joseph: *Clinical Psychological Tests in Psychiatric and Medical Practice.* Springfield, Thomas, 1969.
5. Halpern, Florence: The Bender visual motor gestalt test. In Anderson, Harold H., and Anderson, G. L.: *An Introduction to Projective Techniques.* New York, Prentice-Hall, 1951 [Anderson-Halpern].
6. Hammer, Emanuel F. (Ed.): *Clinical Application of Projective Drawings.* Springfield, Thomas, 1963 [Hammer].
7. Hutt, Max L.: *The Hutt Adaptation of the Bender-Gestalt Test,* 2nd ed., New York, Grune, 1969 [Hutt, 1969].
8. Hutt, Max L., and Briskin, G. J.: *The Hutt Adaptation of the Bender-Gestalt Test.* New York, Grune, 1960 [Hutt-Briskin].
9. Klopfer, Bruno, Ainsworth, Mary, Klopfer, Walter G., and Holt, Robert R.: *Developments in the Rorschach Technique.* New York, Harcourt, 1956, vols. I and II [Klopfer-Developments I and Klopfer-Developments II].
10. Klopfer, Bruno, and Davidson, Helen H.: *Rorschach Technique: An Introductory Manual.* New York, Harcourt, 1962 [Klopfer-Davidson].
11. Machover, Karen: Drawing of the human figure: A method of personality investigation. In Anderson, Harold H., and Anderson, G. L.: *An Introduction to Projective Techniques.* New York, Prentice-Hall, 1951 [Anderson-Machover].
12. Machover, Karen. *Personality Projection in the Drawing of the Human Figure: A Method of Personality Investigation.* Springfield, Thomas, 1965 [Machover].
13. Mayman, Martin, Schafer, Roy, and Rapaport, David: Interpretation of the Wechsler-Bellevue Intelligence Scale in personality appraisal. In Anderson, Harold H., and Anderson, G. L.: *An Introduction to Projective Techniques.* New York, Prentice-Hall, 1951 [Anderson-Mayman-Schafer-Rapaport].
14. Phillips, Leslie, and Smith, Joseph G.: *Rorschach Interpretation: Advanced Technique.* New York, Grune, 1953 [Phillips and Smith].
15. Rapaport, David, Gilland, Merton M., and Schafer, Roy: *Diagnostic Psychological Testing.* New York, Int. Univ., 1968, revised edition edited by Robert R. Holt [Rapaport].

16. Rorschach, Hermann: *Psychodiagnostics,* 5th ed., New York, Grune, 1951 [Rorschach-*Psychodiagnostics*].

17. Schafer, Roy. *Clinical Application of Psychological Tests.* New York, Int. Univ., 1948 [Schafer-Clinical Application].

18. Schafer, Roy. *Psychoanalytic Interpretation in Rorschach Testing.* New York, Grune, 1954 [Schafer-Rorschach].

19. Tolor, Alexander, and Schulberg, Herbert C.: *Evaluation of the Bender-Gestalt Test.* Springfield, Thomas, 1963 [Tolor-Schulberg].

APPENDIX
Rorschach Symbols and Symbol Equivalents

Component	Beck	Klopfer	Phillips and Smith
Whole Response	W	W, W̊	W
Common Details	D	D, d	D
Uncommon Details	Dd	dr, dd, de, di	Dd
Space	Ws, Ds, Dds	S	Ws, Ds, Dds
Form	F+, F, F-	F+, F, F-	F+, F-
Human Movement	M	M	M
Animal Movement	[Animals in Humanlike actions scored M]	FM	FM
Object Movement	Excluded	Fm	Fm
Form Dominant Color	FC	FC	FC
Form Secondary Color	CF	CF	CF
Pure Color	C	C	C
Form Dominant Shading	FY	FC', Fk	FC', Fk
Form Secondary Shading	YF	KF, kF, C'F	KF, kF, C'F
Pure Shading	Y	K, C'	K, C'
Form Dominant Texture	FT	Fc	Fc
Form Secondary Texture	TF	cF	cF
Pure Texture	T	c	c
Form Dominant Vista	FV	FK	FV
Form Secondary Vista	VF	Excluded	VF
Pure Vista	V	Excluded	V

Note: 1) For the sake of clarity, doble content categories under the Beck system are separated in the text with a period (i.e., Human. Religion) rather than with the comma employed by Beck for this purpose.

2) Beck's *Alphabet* category is excluded from the content listing, and the author's *Symbol* is used as a more inclusive category. Phillips and Smith's *Stain* and *War* are employed as additional categories to Beck's. Klopfer categories utilized, not included in Beck but utilized in Phillips and Smith, are *Animal Movement* (FM), *Object Movement* (Fm), Emblem (Em), and Inhuman Human (H). The category *Anal* is also utilized by the author as perhaps more representative of a number of responses that do not seem entirely appropriate under the categories of *Anatomy, Human Detail,* or *Sex*

Index